NEVER DRINK COFFEE DURING
A BUSINESS MEETING

NEVER
DRINK COFFEE
DURING A BUSINESS
MEETING

INSIDER ADVICE FROM A TOP FEMALE CEO

LIZA MARIE GARCIA

New York

NEVER DRINK COFFEE DURING A BUSINESS MEETING
INSIDER ADVICE FROM A TOP FEMALE CEO

Published in New York, New York, by Morgan James Publishing. Morgan James and The Entrepreneurial Publisher are trademarks of Morgan James, LLC. www.MorganJamesPublishing.com

The Morgan James Speakers Group can bring authors to your live event. For more information or to book an event visit The Morgan James Speakers Group at www.TheMorganJamesSpeakersGroup.com.

A free eBook edition is available with the purchase of this print book.

CLEARLY PRINT YOUR NAME ABOVE IN UPPER CASE

Instructions to claim your free eBook edition:
1. Download the BitLit app for Android or iOS
2. Write your name in **UPPER CASE** on the line
3. Use the BitLit app to submit a photo
4. Download your eBook to any device

ISBN 978-1-63047-648-9 paperback
ISBN 978-1-63047-650-2 eBook
ISBN 978-1-63047-649-6 hardcover
Library of Congress Control Number:
2015907154

Cover Design by:
Rachel Lopez
www.r2cdesign.com

Interior Design by:
Bonnie Bushman
The Whole Caboodle Graphic Design

In an effort to support local communities and raise awareness and funds, Morgan James Publishing donates a percentage of all book sales for the life of each book to Habitat for Humanity Peninsula and Greater Williamsburg

Get involved today, visit
www.MorganJamesBuilds.com

Habitat
for Humanity®
Peninsula and
Greater Williamsburg
Building Partner

DEDICATION

This book is dedicated to my lovely, talented and brilliant daughters Julia and Olivia Byrne-Garcia. I wrote this book for them as I do everything in my life for them. My greatest hope is that someday they'll say that I was their most important mentor. I've tried to live my life in a manner worthy of their emulation, to be both mother and mentor. I hope they will remember me in the end with just one word; Love. This is the underlying motivation for everything I do. They are truly my greatest inspiration!

TABLE OF CONTENTS

FOREWORD

I met Liza Garcia in the early 1990's. Liza was brought on board as part of a seven-state telecommunications installation project team. The company I worked for, ROLM, was sold to IBM in 1984. After spending years learning how to do business the 'IBM way', the ROLM telecom group's ownership was being transitioned to Siemens AG's enterprise telecom business unit. With our new business cards in hand we had just completed several successful years revamping the telecom side of the Fred Myer superstores. Siemens-ROLM Communications and my installation team were hoping to repeat our success with the Bon Marché stores account we'd just landed.

Liza was the new kid on the block; young, and untried in the eyes of the rest of the battle-hardened crew. They'd been on the road for two years and were used to relying on one another as a team. From day one, Liza exhibited a passion to excel and a drive to succeed.

Before long, Liza became an invaluable member of the team. She proved she was capable of taking responsibilities above and beyond those she'd been hired to perform. With very little direction, she took ownership of her success and focused her efforts on the team's goals. Liza was self-confident in her ability to hold herself accountable for independent decisions. She stood by them even when her opinion differed from that of management. It comes as no surprise to find Liza has become a CEO.

In this book, Liza has taken the strategies she's learned over the years and placed them in an easy to follow format with emphasis on her own insights regarding the social and emotional characteristics needed for success. I believe everyone can benefit from reading chapters four and five as these chapters deal with overcoming fears, understanding strategies, dealing with emotions and conflicts as well as resolution techniques. It is no secret that there are more men in positions of authority than women. Learn to deal with them.

Golf, as mentioned in chapter nine, is a sport well worth cultivating. Many interviews, promotions and ideas get tossed while on the fairway. Golf can be your friend. If you can't get the handle of hitting the ball, make yourself indispensable by driving the cart, or by learning the clubs and being a caddy to one of the decision makers. Do anything that will make you "one of the boys" and keep you in the forefront alongside your male competition.

For some reading this book, you may be at the start of your career. For others, you may be reading this because your career is stalled and you don't feel you have anywhere to go or anyone to go to. Heed the advice given in chapter twelve as well as throughout several different chapters as Liza has given examples of attributes and traits that are important for success. It is essential you cultivate and incorporate them into your daily life until they become habit. Not sure how to do this? Not comfortable doing that? Then practice, practice, and practice.

If you haven't done so, take a Sociology course. It will open your eyes to the development of social relationships, interaction and collective behavior. I found that out of all my many degrees and certifications, my lone Sociology course taken back in the 1970s turned out to be the most valuable resource for success both in and outside of business.

Liza gives sound advice when she encourages you to step into other people's shoes and walk around for a day, viewing life from someone else's perspective rather than your own. You must find your own identity by learning to connect with others, communicate and channel your drive and belief in your own abilities. Surround yourself with successful people, male and female and above all, be patient. Remember, it may take years or even an entire career to polish and hone your leadership skills.

After retiring from the corporate world of telecommunications I became a nurse. I currently work in the field of corrections. A few months ago I was the recipient of a State of Colorado Department of Corrections Challenge Coin. The Challenge Coin was awarded in appreciation for my part in saving the life of a young offender who suffered a major heart attack while playing handball. During the award ceremony, the presenter noted the Director of Prisons had never received such an outpouring of letters over an incident. These letters weren't from management or staff but from the inmates who watched from their windows and cells as resuscitation was performed on one of their own. What surprised them the most was how our rescue team never gave up even after the young man stopped breathing and his pulse was lost. The inmates wrote that they couldn't believe that staff cared, one way or another, about saving a prisoner. How grateful they were to know someone cared about whether they lived or died.

Jim Stovall, a renowned motivational speaker has been quoted as saying "you need to be aware of what others are doing, applaud their efforts, acknowledge their successes, and encourage them in their own pursuits. When we all help one another, everybody wins." Just as this story goes to show, there is someone always watching. So give your best every day.

Liza's final chapter discusses achieving balance and finding purpose, being in transition, anticipating change and mentoring. The entire book is chock-full of observations and helpful hints to support and elevate women in the workplace and allow them to take their rightful place in upper management.

Liza's book is long overdue and it's a joy to see her passing on what she's learned to the next generation of women in the workforce. If even one woman reaches down and helps another succeed because something in this book inspires her, it will be like the butterfly whose fluttering wing sets off a hurricane.

There is no doubt that for Liza, writing this book was a labor of love.

—**Robyn Button**, MSN, MBA, RN, FNP

PREFACE:
A NOTE FROM THE CEO

"Without ambition one starts nothing. Without work one finishes nothing. The prize will not be sent to you. You have to win it."
—Ralph Waldo Emerson

I hail from among the slowly growing ranks of female CEO's who have started and successfully run their own companies in fields long dominated by men. In 1994, I started one of the first telecommunications software design companies in the nation. From the very first days of my company, I have not only championed my own cause as a woman, but those of all my female counterparts. Being a woman has never stood in my way in business.

In this book, I will focus on one of the greatest resources to your career: the bold women who've gone before you in business and their infinite wisdom. I also attribute my success in business to rising to embrace change when it has come to me, but also to actively inviting change all the way along. Here in this book, I present my advice on how to harness the power of change by utilizing all the resources you can.

Looking back to the days when my company was in its infancy, a pivotal event stands out; the day when one of my primary vendors came to me and asked me to "attempt" to provide something different than the hourly pricing method we'd been using to price my company's services. He asked me to make a huge change and develop something that would be more of what was described as a "not to exceed bid" pricing model. So I developed and trialed a new pricing method and, not long afterward, it was adopted as an industry standard for telecommunications as well as other industries. This new bidding model provided a way for our client's to keep their costs down because it allowed vendors to budget the pricing they in turn offered their own customers.

Responding to this particular challenge meant I needed to know how to price all our services. It also required my knowledge of how to efficiently manage every area of those services; the administration piece, the database engineer role and the training services, or my company would lose money. Men traditionally filled many of these roles. The pricing model I developed was new to the industry, and so was the idea that a woman could have thought of it. Yet, I did.

I believe this type of challenge and the way I responded to it by inviting the change is the reason my company has become very efficient at what it does. Since then, backed by my team of employees, I've often been able to develop processes well before my competitors. At times my company has even developed software solutions quicker than those of our billion-dollar vendors who certainly have more resources. These early experiences and others like it prepared and shaped me. They shaped and developed my company. However, none of this happened overnight.

Before starting my own business, I spent time in the trenches of corporate America. I paid my dues, playing strictly by the rules and taking orders from managers who were usually men. As my career progressed, I did benefit from the influence of a few extraordinary female managers. They were tremendously helpful to me by providing the insider's knowledge I needed to sustain and obtain all of my endeavors. However, I could not help but notice those exemplary women represented a pretty thin contingent.

My purpose in writing this book originates from the observation that even today, some 20 years into my career, there are still too few women aspiring to and ascending to top management positions. Lately, I've become increasingly concerned that although the number of women graduating from colleges and universities is growing, the number of women already working in top business positions to guide them is at best only holding steady, and possibly even shrinking.

This absence of high-ranking female leadership in business creates and perpetuates an environment where the young women who enter the workforce today face a real disadvantage when it comes to getting the support they need to advance their careers. Without this invaluable guidance, men will forever dominate business. The young women entering business today need an action plan or they won't be able to benefit from the same kind of mentoring relationships I did. With so few readily available, female role models and mentor-guides available they will need to be deliberately sought ought.

So here is my offer to those of you just starting out: I'll be your first mentor. I've written this book to help fill the gap in leadership and to deliver to you the all-important information you'll need to establish more mentoring relationships like the ones that have been key to my success. I'll share with you the lessons I have learned. I'll provide you with a toolkit I've assembled myself and packed with the advice of other great women who have gone before you. I'll teach you how to adopt an attitude of not just anticipating change but inviting it into your work-life.

ALL SUCCESSFUL WOMEN HAVE AN UNSTOPPABLE DRIVE

"Nothing can stop the man with the right mental attitude from achieving his goal; nothing on earth can help the man with the wrong mental attitude."
—Thomas Jefferson

Yesterday I hired a "fledgling" trainer and I think she is going to work out great. As I went through the process of considering her and the other applicants, I narrowed down the outstanding traits for success that I've found in each of my best engineers and trainers.

Here is a list of those traits:

1

- Enthusiasm
- Openness to life and work change
- Willingness to do things even if they are below her job description (like getting clients coffee or making copies)
- Ability to handle multiple jobs/multiple projects simultaneously
- Positive Attitude
- Creativity—the ability to come up with new innovative ideas, or a new approach
- An Unstoppable Work Ethic—to work as hard as it takes, no matter what until the job is done

These are great traits but the one that makes an applicant truly stand out is her drive. You either have it or you don't. I don't know exactly where drive comes from. I've hired (and fired) many employees who had fantastic resumes and interviewed well. They came from good backgrounds and seemed to have had a quality education but in the end they had no ambition. They had no drive in their personal careers, no drive to be the best software engineers for our company and really no drive to satisfy our clients to their utmost. I've learned that unfortunately drive isn't anything I can motivate or provide a company program to incubate. In my observation, people either have it or they don't.

I'm going to assume that you have that drive! I have no doubt that if you picked up this book, you do. You are keenly interested in being successful in business and you are already committed to doing whatever it takes to achieve your goals. It's my goal to assist you in making that happen. I'm not going to tell you how to motivate yourself; I'm going to tell you how to take what you already have going for you and teach you how to apply the inside information I am going to give you so you can benefit from my experience as a CEO.

Many of us, myself included, still come from a generation when our mothers, if they were ever in business, were just making the first tiny footprints across the thresholds of Corporate America. The success of the next generation, you, depends on those of us who have gone before you sharing our knowledge. I'll do this for you. I'm ready to bring you on board.

Where Does Your Drive Come From?
I know Where I Got Mine...

I was born and raised in Salt Lake City, Utah. Both my parents are Mexican Americans. You might assume they speak Spanish but they do not because in their era parents were sensitive to making sure their kids were 100% assimilated. Here is an example of where my family embraced changed and adapted to fit the culture of their new country. It's this tradition of inviting change and adaptation that has made my family successful in business.

My grandparents on both sides were also born in Utah. Some of them worked as manual laborers. My dad grew up without the regular presence of his father. Fortunately he had a resourceful and determined mother, my grandmother Julia Garcia, who, despite her lack of education, was uncompromising in her vision of a better future for her children. Born in 1919, Julia lived to the wonderful age of 93. She certainly wasn't an executive but she knew that the key to her family's future lay in her managing her family by inviting change into their lives and rejecting the notion that things would or should remain as they were. She knew that education was the path to this change and she encouraged my father and his siblings to go to college.

My father, Manuel T. Garcia, "Manny," earned a Bachelor's degree in Business Administration from Westminster College in Salt Lake City Utah. He was a Manager for AT&T and Harris 3M for many years and retired as the Director of Communications for the University of Utah Medical Center. My mother also earned a bachelor's degree from Westminster College. Both my parents were the first college graduates in their immediate families. While I was growing up there was never a doubt that my sister and I would also graduate from college. That value and that expectation was very clearly communicated to us and so it became our goal.

Fortunate Influences at a Tender Age

"Dance makes you fearless, putting yourself and your personal expression out there for the world to judge, it takes a certain type of person to do that."
—**Misty Copeland**

Like many little girls, I was lucky to have been afforded dance classes. Unlike many little girls, I was fortunate to have had an extremely special, world-renowned dance teacher, none other than "the" Virginia Tanner who established the Tanner Dance Program in Utah in 1937. My selfless mother drove my sister and me from the mountains of East Salt Lake City to the dance studio, which was located quite far away. She did this several times weekly from when I was three until I was a teenager.

I don't know how my mom found out about the program. My mother's upbringing was quite different and definitely not privileged. I'm sure the classes were a financial sacrifice for my parents. I remember that my mother sometimes helped out by sewing some of the costumes for our performances. This demonstrated to me how deeply my mother was committed to our success. It was what all the involved mothers did. Like my grandmother, my mother invited this change, invited the new with no possible way of knowing just where or how far it would take us.

Virginia Tanner was recognized internationally as a pioneer of children's dance and as one of its finest teachers. In her heyday some said that Salt Lake City was the most blessed city in the world to have the world's master children's dance teacher and that no other place, including New York, London, Paris, or Moscow, had anyone who could touch her genius for teaching children what was called the "exciting purity of the dancing arts." The Tanner Dance Program is now an arts auxiliary of the College of Fine Arts at the University of Utah.

Miss Virginia, as we called her, had a profound effect on me and on all of the dancers. When Miss Virginia walked into the dance studio, we all stood up straighter, pointed our toes harder we all learned to hold ourselves in a dancer's carriage. I remember being afraid to breathe in her presence.

Miss Virginia had an indescribable ability to command instant respect. I'm not quite sure exactly how she did it. I can't reduce it to a look, a movement or anything she said, but you knew it was there, felt it was there and that was astounding. As I have grown in my career and as a business owner, this is an ability I've strived to capture for myself. She was the first woman I wanted to emulate. I knew this at a very young age.

Miss Virginia took special notice of me when I was in my very first dance class at the age three. She declared me a "child of dance." From then on I was extended great privileges. I traveled with the Children's Dance Theater (her modern dance

Company) to Canada, and across the United States. I got to do pieces like "Water Study" and other advanced Martha Graham style pieces.

Wherever we went, I was always the youngest of the troupe. When I was seven years old, I was actually invited along to dance at the Kennedy Center in Washington, DC. It was a simply amazing experience and it certainly expanded my horizons and made all things seem possible. It was on one of these trips I had a second strike of great fortune.

One Blessed Encounter Leads to Another

The second fortunate mentor from my childhood is a woman I now call "Nana," Gloria Castano. Gloria was, among other things, the National Program Director of The Sacred Dance Guild in Severna, Maryland from 1972 to 1980. With Sacred Dance Gloria produced week-long inter-faith dance Festivals in Boston, Denver, San Antonio and Miami. Gloria is an alumnus of Jacob's Pillow, a national landmark center and dance school located in the Berkshire Mountains of Massachusetts, where she completed her study in 1957.

Following this period, she enjoyed 10 years of international performance in theaters and on the concert stage. After a year of performance in Europe in 1962, she returned to the United States and began a teaching career that has spanned more than 50 years. Most recently she is known for her work with the

Senior Performing Group "Skyloom" an interfaith and inter-generational dance group from the greater Boston area. She is well-respected and admired in her own right and has had numerous achievements and credits in her dance career.

In Gloria's own words:

"I met Liza in October of 1975 in Washington D.C. Her dance teacher, Virginia Tanner, was my dear friend. Many students from her dance school in Salt Lake City were in Washington as part of the educational and performing arts offerings for the 1976 Bi-Centennial. I had traveled to D.C. with a few young students of my own to see Virginia and the performances. That's when I met Liza who was just seven years of age at the time."

When it was time for the Tanner School's demonstrations, the room was suddenly filled with two dozen little dancers all under the age of 12. Each wore a pastel-colored leotard and each was adorned with a Lucite pendant twisted into the shape of a dancer. As part of this special dance, the children twirled, jumped, stretched and soared through the air enchanting everyone. When the music came to a quieting end, each of the children found someone in the audience, danced to their side, took off the necklace and encircled it around their neck. Liza came to me. It was in that moment that we found each other.

The events of this long weekend were joy-filled beyond description. Liza and I shared a glance here, and word or two there, as the days went on and when it came time for good-byes, we found ourselves in the same elevator. There, Liza handed me a note with a four-leaf clover necklace. I still have both of the necklaces she gave me and I treasure them. Reflecting, I recognize how, in these simple acts, this courageous little girl demonstrated such a natural confidence. It was she who pursued our relationship by calling and sending me letters. Going after what she wants is simply second nature to Liza. This characteristic is a tribute to her early and present achievements. She determines a path and its place on her journey and time and again claims her victories."

I came to know Gloria when on that trip to DC, as she mentions. I remember that I became so fond of her on the trip that I gave her that 4-leaf clover necklace. I have no idea where I got the necklace. The only thing I do recall talking about then was that since she was a little "brown" like me (she is Italian), perhaps I felt some kinship with her. I learned later that she had no children of her own. That initial connection allowed us to discover our common ground and to develop a rich relationship.

Imagine me, a little girl from Utah, hearing Gloria's stories about performing in places such as Thule, Greenland where it was sunny 24 hours a day. And of Sicily, where her own family was from, and of concerts in a lavish casino in Switzerland,

and supper clubs in Rome, Milan and Florence. I remember one particular story she told me about a charity event at the "Casino Municipale di Sanremo," the oldest casino in Italy famous for its music festivals, where the featured artist was an accomplished jazz pianist who was Romano Mussolini, the son of Bonito Mussolini, *the* Italian Prime Minister and the first of 20th century Europe's fascist dictators who was married to Sofia Loren's sister! Such sweet and exciting memories Gloria shared with me. She fascinated me and broadened my world view exponentially.

From this chance meeting began our lifelong friendship and a "family" relationship. When I was in my early teens, she became my godmother. She was an important part of my wedding. She has visited our family numerous times. She is today known "Nana," to both of my girls and she is a significant part of our lives.

Gloria, today, remains absolutely unbelievable in her beauty, her poise and in the love she continues to share. Absolutely everyone she has ever taught remains so grateful to her for the liberal sharing of her talents. She is still healthy and amazing today. Like Virginia Tanner, Gloria is also one of those women who walks in a room and immediately commands respect. I attribute the early influence of these two amazing women—and, of course, that of my parents— to fostering my belief that I was and remain capable of great things. These are the women who demonstrated to me the limitless potential of *all* women. They were the women who were pushing the boundaries and expanding the opportunities for all of us who came after them. These two women, along with many of their generation are so deserving of our remembrance and respect.

Type "A" All the Way

So there I was at seven, already believing I could take on the world. I attended a private, Catholic School through fifth grade. When I was entering sixth grade, I begged my parents to put me in a public school for my middle school years. I excelled there. My first year, I was elected homeroom president. After that, I ran for class president. This required giving a speech in front of the whole student body. I barely remember that speech. I didn't win but instead of discouraging me it motivated me to try harder. I recognized that I had an inner drive that set me apart from my classmates. In reaching and falling short of my goal, I learned to be persistent. I began setting my own course, learning very early in my life that I am a leader and not a follower.

In high school I kept setting and reaching for new goals. I sang in the choir. I wondered why I didn't win all the voice competitions I entered. I was a member of the Utah Youth Symphony at age 14 and was never happy with my 5th, 6th or

7th chair positions when I was not First Violin. I became a JV cheerleader my sophomore year of high school, the first year I tried out, and I wondered why I didn't make varsity. I was elected the co-captain of the JV squad that first year but it really wasn't good enough for me. By junior year, I was a Varsity cheerleader and I was winning awards at cheerleading camps. I was never satisfied and always seeking to move up. I also played classical piano at age 7 and classical violin at age 9 through the very strict Suzuki method.

To say I was an over-achiever and highly involved was an understatement. I always believed I was special. I believed I could do anything if I worked hard enough at it and that I *deserved* to be able to do anything. My parents, Miss Virginia and Ms. Gloria all showed me that there were "no limits" to my capacity and I believed it wholeheartedly.

Perhaps you are seeing a lot of yourself in my story. Can you identify the source of your own drive? Reflecting back on how far you've come is very useful when planning where you're going. How can you measure your success without an appreciation for what you've been through to get where you are? Take a moment now, close your eyes and think back through something that was tough in your past, at any age, something that is a difficult memory and remember how you came through it. Once you do this you will gain insight into yourself and into the origins of your own drive.

My Childhood Primed Me for Business

"Her calm, soft spoken and understated demeanor belies her strength of conviction and clarity of thought."
—**Chandra Kochar**

My ambitions have mostly focused me outside the home. In fact I can't cook and I didn't want to get married until later in life. I had no plans to be married before age 30. For me college and then career was my complete focus. I was accepted to Assumption College in Massachusetts. I was devastated like a spoiled teenager when my parents told me they couldn't afford it. So I attended the University of Utah. It was not my first choice but it was an equally fine institution. I decided to give it my all. Following in my dad's footsteps, I earned an undergraduate degree in business administration.

My junior year at the University, I responded to a posting for an internship at IBM. I applied for it, interviewed and was hired at an IBM owned company called ROLM Systems, their telecommunications company. In 1984, Bell Telephone Company was forced to divest itself, creating seven competitor companies known as the "Baby Bells." This opened the door to any other data processing company that wanted to enter the voice communications industry. ROLM, a competitor to the Baby Bell companies, was purchased by IBM during the breakup. It was here that I met and worked under Kathy Dunn, my very first manager in corporate America. She was the best manager I could have ever hoped for as a young, college woman just starting out.

I remember Kathy was always impeccably dressed. She held herself with an air of managerial authority, that same quality I'd observed in Virginia Tanner and Gloria Castano when I was a child. What I also observed about Kathy was that when she attended conference meetings that often became loud and boisterous (with what I refer to now as "everyone's ego talking") she would sit quietly and listen intently. Then, when a pause in the conversation came, or when her input was solicited, she would speak. The entire room would quiet down and listen. To me, it seemed like she chose her words carefully and always had something important to say. Her presence compelled respect.

Kathy probably had no idea that I thought of her as a mentor. She most definitely was. Later during my internship I applied for a Contracts Administrator position. I had little experience or qualifications for the job and I didn't get it. Kathy managed my let down with such gentleness, at the same time making sure I knew that she noticed and appreciated me and my willingness to reach for something greater even at my young age.

When the summer was ending and my internship at IBM was coming to end, I was asked to attend a meeting with the

Engineering Manager. Her name was Marti Heskamp. Marti told me that there was an opening for a voice engineer and they wanted to offer me full-time employment. At that point I had about forty hours left to earn my degree. Marti told me that they would pay for the rest of my classes if I would accept the position. So I changed my schedule to night classes and took the job. Within a week of my employment they had flown me to the IBM/ROLM training center in Santa Clara California. It was there I trained to become a software design engineer. My career had begun!

Student to Businesswoman

"If you're offered a seat on a rocket ship, don't ask what seat. Just get on."
—Sheryl Sandberg

When I was 24 and still just a few years into my career as a Telecom Systems Engineer, I was working as the Lead Software Engineer on a particularly large project. This project had been going south for about a year. All problems seemed to be coming to a head. It was unraveling so badly that the project manager literally checked into the hospital to have a mental breakdown!

At that same time all of this was happening, my direct manager decided to go on vacation! She seemed completely oblivious to the complications we were facing on the project. In addition to her inattention, she criticized me about why I was working hundred-hour work weeks! As her "help" toward the project, she actually presented me a card for a spa package. While she may have seen that as a nice gesture, what I needed was her leadership and project management. I didn't need pampering! I never used that gift card.

Meanwhile our client, IBM/Siemens, was flying in engineers from around the country to save the project. Unfortunately, now it was up to me to coordinate all their work on top of my own. At that point I really didn't feel experienced enough to handle both the project management work and the customer issues.

When Thanksgiving came I was told to cancel my approved vacation to see *my* family in Salt Lake City because all the other engineers were going to be off-site with *their* families. That was my "last straw." The camel's back was broken and as impetuous as it may sound I quit my plum first job with IBM.

There I was, 24 and starting again. I had no savings and I left not even knowing if I'd get the cash from my retirement fund. What I did know was that I was young, ambitious and driven with the talent and skills to be successful. When my immediate manager failed to perform her job, I quit in response. I had not yet learned what I know now: when one level of management doesn't get it, go above them. In other words, escalate, escalate and escalate.

What happened next? I created a new job for myself by calling the 10 telecommunications company in the phone book. Yes, the Yellow Pages. There was no internet at that time. I faxed my resume to all of them. One company, Duracomm, called me back. The next thing I knew, I was a project manager for a data and telecom company and learning outside/inside plant and data networks. In this organizational structure I reported directly to the CEO, Mr. Duran. I became the only project manager for Duracomm.

My Rocket Ship Seat

"She had two prospects: Total Failure or Vast Success."
—Elizabeth Holmes

I had been working at Duracomm for less than six months when out-of-the-blue my former *boss's* boss at IBM called me. He said that he was sorry that I had quit and that he wished that I had escalated my grievance to him instead of leaving. He also said that they had a new client Bon Marche (Macy's, Inc.) with 56 locations across the United States and they wanted *me* to come back to work for Siemens (IBM had bought Siemens) as a Software Engineer doing exactly what I was doing before!

This new client would be *mine* completely. I'd be working for myself with a huge increase in pay. This was a defining moment in my career. They put me on the spot to make my decision within a few hours. The project kick off meeting was that next morning in Spokane, Washington, where I was expected to present my installation strategy to the client. If I agreed to the assignment, I'd need to fly out that day! So of course I said yes!

I continued working as an independent contractor for a while. Then, in 1994 I started my own company, Byrne Integrated Communications (BIC), and hired several employees. I continued to grow and nurture my team. The business, expanded to two offices, one outside Portland Oregon the other in Seattle Washington. My businesses continued to grow successfully for the next 15 years. In addition to Siemens, our client included companies like NIKE, NASA and many of the Fortune 100/500 companies in between.

Field Notes

At BIC, we kept up with our telecommunications and technical certifications in whatever way was needed to keep current in the industry. This was a lofty endeavor and quite difficult. As a small business, sometimes this meant asking a customer to "sponsor" us. Sometimes it meant pretending to be customers to the education center. This was key to our longevity in being able to provide our software design engineering services to Siemens and their clients. In technology, if you aren't certified in the latest technology platform, you are left behind.

Another one of our strategies was to commit to bringing constant change to BIC. As Siemens changed, we adapted. As Siemens identified their weaknesses to us we quickly filled their gaps and cover their "issues" with our services. Our focus was on keeping in step with them month after month, quarter after quarter so they would always look to us to fulfill their labor shortcomings. More than that, we strove to build processes better and more efficiently than Siemens. While we were at it, we found a way to not just build a better mousetrap, but we found a way to make it more profitable. In fact, on any given day, I can point to a number of processes or deliverables that were developed due to the idea of differentiating ourselves from our competitors or filling a need of our end users or clients.

Our focus was and remains trained on meeting the needs of each of our clients and each of our vendors. When they say "jump" we jump and don't waste time asking "how high?" This is what has made my team and me successful and it's also what has caused us to routinely beat out our competitors. We never take it for granted that your first customer will be your last if you aren't careful as an organization.

The Takeaway

So this is my story and the story of the two companies I founded. As you will read more about specifically in the next chapter, women are still so under-represented in the upper ranks of corporate America. You need women like me who have "made it" in business to share what we know. You need to hear more stories like mine. We will take a look at the state of affairs of women in business peppered with some ideas on how to improve things for our collective future.

CONGRATULATIONS, YOU'VE
GOT YOUR DEGREE! NOW WHAT?

"Graduation is only a concept. In real life every day you graduate. Graduation is a process that goes on until the last day of your life. If you can grasp that, you'll make a difference."

—Arie Pencovici

It's no small accomplishment to earn an undergraduate or graduate degree in business. Congratulations! Women now achieve 40% of all the MBA's granted each year in the US. So, what can you expect next? Well, the good news is that there are more opportunities for young women entering today's workplace than ever before. The bad news is that the business world can still be mighty unfriendly to women, at least in comparison to what young male graduates experience.

Let's consider the wage gap between women and men with business degrees. "It isn't very significant when you're just starting out and usually it corresponds to grades and course selection," says Marianne Bertrand, an Economics Professor at the University Of Chicago School Of Business, citing results of studies on female compensation among women with MBA's. But women still earn just a fraction of what men earn for comparable jobs. Bertrand says what's even more striking is how much that gap grows over time." (Demast, Alison. "MBA wage gap between men, women grows." SFGate May 8, 2104. Accessed February 28, 2015. http://www.sfgate.com/business/article/MBA-wage-gap-between-men-women-grows-4153232.php)

According to this and other studies, women were better off 10 years ago. "Today the pay gap among graduates of elite business schools is widening. Where we were once on near-equal footing, female graduates now earn between 79 and 93% for every dollar paid to their male counterparts. In a study by Catalyst—a non-profit group that focuses on expanding opportunities for women in business—female MBA's are paid on average $4,600 less than in their early jobs than men and the figure grows to $30,000 by mid-career." (Lang, Ilene. "Take 5:

The MBA Pay Gap." May 23, 2011. Accessed February, 2014. http://www.catalyst.org/blog/catalyzing/take-5-mba-pay-gap). This should be making you angry. If it doesn't, stop reading!

Why is this? If women are graduating in *greater* numbers from business schools, how come we aren't *earning* more in the workforce? If you've just graduated, likely you've heard about this in your business program. There are many factors that affect and contribute to wage disparity. Women leaving the workforce is a big one. Not earning the same pay as our male counterparts is a huge disincentive. No wonder women stop working. This is infuriating to me.

So how do we start to fix it? We will never achieve parity if we don't stay in the workforce. We've got to stay in, in larger numbers, and we've got be successful. Not just in achieving wage parity but in offering women ways of accommodating both career and family. Things will never move forward if business remains dominated by men. History has proven that only women will take up and fight for our own causes.

These are the tough issues all career women face at some point. I certainly don't have all of the answers but I can tell you what's worked for me. I have always had a nanny. I hired her with the same amount of diligence and scrutiny that I give all my new hires. I knew instinctively that this employee would be one of the most important positions I'd ever hire. I've also always had a very hands-on approach to her care of my daughters. I plan the menus for them and orchestrate their daily activities based on themes and strict requirements that include certain time for things such as reading and the arts. I have always encouraged them to participate in team sports.

I have been fortunate to find a wonderful young woman, Lauren Kulver. She has become an integral part of our family. Her dedication to and love for my children has enabled me to pursue my career relentlessly. Over the years, she's become completely devoted to my children and I trust her implicitly. Other working women have chosen to utilize day care and the assistance of family members to manage the responsibility that having children brings. It's a choice to delegate this important responsibility to someone else but it can be done if building a career is what you want or need to do.

I could write a whole book about managing a career and family and still not provide a solution that would adequately suit everyone and I don't want to start another episode of the "Mommy Wars." It seems to me that we haven't found the perfect balance for families yet, whether mom is in the workplace or staying at home. So let's just agree to work towards it together. These issues are intensely personal.

For now, let's assume you *are* a career woman in for the long haul. You *do* want to become a top executive. You want to be a CEO. You want a stellar career and you aren't daunted by the fact that you'll likely have to work harder for less pay as a woman and that you'll probably have to pay a large portion of what you earn to cover child care if you start a family. So let's focus on the absence of female role models and mentors in the workforce because this is one we can make headway on right now. We must seek out and take advantage of the women who *are* there in the business world.

Field Notes

I'll guide you. I've been there. I know what it's like. In business school, you probably found yourself surrounded by bright and ambitious women who were ready to take on the world. As you step forward along your career you will find yourself wondering where all those women went. Your contemporaries from school won't be alongside you for very long in the workforce, they weren't in mine. You won't find many women to look up to in the ranks of upper or executive management, I haven't. As we have established, the business world is still largely dominated by men. You're going to need more than your business school could teach you to succeed.

The Takeaway

Here is where our journey together begins. As a woman and a CEO, I'm going to step in as your role model and offer you my mentoring so we can work together to stack the odds a bit more in your favor. We'll focus on how to find great mentors of your own so you can take advantage of the multitude of opportunities that yet abound for smart women. First we'll take a look at some of the facts about women in the workforce and then we'll look at where you'll fit in and I'll give you everything I've learned on my journey to becoming CEO. I did it. So can you!

WELCOME TO THE WORLD OF WOMEN IN BUSINESS, YOU'RE GONNA BE LONELY!

"The Blunt Truth is that men still run the world and I'm not sure that's going so well."
—Sheryl Sandberg

A s a CEO and a woman, I'm not going to kid you: it's tough to look around and see so few female faces in the corporate workforce, both in positions of leadership and in corporate boardrooms. It doesn't have to be this way. You represent the next wave of women who can change things forever, and I want to encourage you to aspire to bringing this change. Women don't have to accept that this is simply the way things are and that it will never change. It's just not true. Women *can* succeed in business and in much greater numbers than they are today. I'm going to teach you how. But let's first have a look at where we stand.

The fact is, women are still definitely underrepresented, especially in Fortune 500 companies. Forbes magazine recently cited a study in the Grant Thornton International Business Report that says, "The proportion of women in senior roles is stuck at 24%, the same as 2013, 2009 and 2007…"(Scott, Mary E. "Number of Women in Senior Management Stuck at 24%." May 6, 2104. Accessed February, 2015. http://www.forbes.com/sites/forbesasia/2014/03/06/number-of-women-in-senior-management-stagnant-at-24/).

According to the website for International Labor Organization (ILO), a special agency of the United Nations, this inequality is a global challenge. "While millions of women have become successful entrepreneurs, women are still grossly underrepresented in the world's board-rooms. Women often have less access to productive resources, education, and skills development and labor market opportunities than men in many societies. Largely, this is because of persistent social norms ascribing gender roles, which are often, slow to change." (http://www.ilo.org/employment/areas/gender-and-employment/lang--en/index.htm).

And it's not just about how fewer women are showing up in boardrooms and corner offices but how women are portrayed in the media. Hollywood movies and TV programs can contribute to a negative, or at least less present, image of women as contributing factors to success.

Film, TV star and founder of the "Institute on Gender in Media" Geena Davis knows firsthand the challenges of being a woman in Hollywood. Davis observes some sobering statistics about why men—and even children—might see women in a negative light. Says Davis, "The basics are that for every one female-speaking character in family-rated films (G, PG and PG-13), there are roughly three male characters. In crowd and group scenes in these films—live-action and animated—only 17 percent female characters; and that the ratio of male to female characters has been exactly the same since 1946… the female characters, they lack occupations and aspirations…you get the picture." (www.seejane.org) Davis advocates for change by the inspiring slogan, "If she can see it, she can be it," calling for more representation of women in media, particularly in roles that portray good roles models to young girls.

So where are the Female Executives?

"When will there be enough women on the court? When there are nine."
—Ruth Bader Ginsburg

So why is it? Why, despite all the advantages we've made through education, understanding, activism and action are women not seen as part of the big picture, let alone the future? To find the answer—and the solution—this chapter will discuss the topic in two parts. First, we'll delve deeper into understanding why women are so underrepresented and then, in practical terms, we'll discuss a variety of methods for reversing that trend—or the better.

Let's start with why. Why aren't there more women in American's boardrooms? Christine Bork, former CEO of YWCA Metropolitan Chicago, contends that American companies simply—and wrongly—don't see women as a good investment. Writing for HuffingtonPost.com, Bork explains, "I believe one solution is to start by speaking the language of business—profits. What many companies fail to realize is that investing in women is good for the bottom line. Companies with the highest representation of women on their top management teams perform better financially than companies with the lowest representation." (Bork, Christine, "Women in

Corporate America." The Huffington Post. August 17, 20111 Accessed February 2015. http://www.huffingtonpost.com/ christine-bork/women-in-corporate-americ_b_858794.html). To me this is huge!

Contributor Kelly Wallace, writing for CNN.com, explains, "Part of the challenge… is convincing male leaders there's not a limited supply of strong female candidates." Wallace, Kelly. "No Movement at the Top in Corporate America." (CNN. December 11, 2013. Accessed February, 2015. http://www. cnn.com/2013/12/11/living/no-change-on-women-board-seats-parents/index.html).

Could it be that we women actually are contributing to the problem? That's the theory supposed by Victoria Pynchon, author of *A is for A**hole: the Grownups' ABCs of Conflict Resolution* (Reason Press, 2010). In an article for Pynchon writes, "The real reason there aren't more women on boards is that there are not enough of us who believe we're qualified to serve." Pynchon points to low self-esteem in women and the lack of articles, editorials and op-ed pieces written by businesswomen as some of the contributing factors and signs of why more women don't rise to leadership status. (Pynchon, Victoria. "The Real Reason there Aren't More Women on Boards." Forbes. June 4, 2012. Accessed February, 2015. http://www.forbes.com/sites/ shenegotiates/2012/06/04/the-real-reason-there-arent-more-women-on-boards/)

Then there is the Leaky Pipe Theory. Never heard of it? Read on: "Catherine Wolfram, an associate professor at UC Berkeley's Haas Business School, studied the "Leaky Pipe" theory, which says that women just aren't staying in corporate positions long enough to rise through the ranks. Her study found that 15 years after graduating from Harvard College, 28 percent of the females who received MBAs were stay-at-home moms, while only 6 percent of those earning medical degrees left their jobs, suggesting the business world is less female-friendly." Swartz, Angela, "Women in Top Positions are Few." (March 16, 2013. SFGate, Accessed February, 2015. http://www.sfgate.com/business/article/Women-in-top-executive-positions-are-few-4360451.php). This causes me to wonder, why isn't an MBA as valuable as a M.D. to the woman earning it? Why is it easier to keep being a doctor than to continue being a businesswoman?

Finally, as again Oscar-winning actress Geena Davis says, "It may be that we are simply not showcasing enough powerful women in film and on TV—where many young women, and even men—begin to form their earliest values and options. We are in effect enculturating kids from the very beginning to see women and girls as not even taking up half of the space. Couldn't it be that the percentage of women in leadership positions in many areas of society—Congress, law partners, Fortune 500 board members, military officers, tenured professors and many more—stall out at around 17 percent because that's the ratio we've come to see as the norm?" (www.seejane.org)

How do you fit in? How Can You Position Yourself?

So let's establish that women still hold only about *one* out of 20 top-management positions in high-profile Fortune 500 corporations and that's only slightly higher than 20 years ago. Hold on, that's pretty bad news. But don't forget that, like me, one in four chief executives running a *small* business is now a woman!

It's unfortunate that as people move up in careers, women start to fall out and leave the workplace far quicker relative to men. Why? It is may be a contributing factor that men gain operations experience *earlier* in their careers and that may qualify them more for the top jobs but it is largely about pay and childcare. Corporate America is still not very accommodating of the needs of women with families. Many now offer time off to care for sick children, working at home and telecommuting, flex-time and on-site day care, for example, but it is still not very widespread. I'll discuss this in detail. But guess what? Other issues plague career women with families besides that of finding childcare coverage during the day and sometimes it's not perpetuated by the men in business, but by women themselves.

Recently, top female executive and journalist Katharine Zaleski issued an apology to working mothers saying, "I scheduled last minute meetings at 4:30pm all of the time. It didn't dawn on me that parents might need to pick up their kids at daycare. I was obsessed with the idea of showing my commitment to the job by staying in the office 'late' even though I wouldn't start working until 10:30 am while parents would come in at 8:30 am. For mothers in the workplace, its death by a thousand cuts—and sometimes other women are holding the knives. I didn't realize this—or how horrible I'd been—until five years later, when I gave birth to a daughter of my own." (Zaleski, Katharine, Female Company President: "I'm Sorry to All the Mothers I worked With" Fortune, March 3, 2015. Accessed March, 2015. (http://fortune.com/2015/03/03/female-company-president-im-sorry-to-all-the-mothers-i-used-to-work-with/). Personally I have to say that motherhood and the added responsibility that it brought to my life did change my own expectation of the time availability of my employees. Once I had children of my own, I understood, first hand, how "off shift" hours could actually promote productivity when I provided it to those in my staff who were parents.

In many cases, in little and big ways, we women are still being forced to choose between caring for our families and tending our careers. Yes, the list of companies that provide on-site child care *is* growing, but slowly. Yes, legislation has been passed to protect women who take maternity leave with the Family Medical Leave Act of 1993 which guarantees us

12 weeks of *unpaid* time but when Australia passed a parental leave law in 2010, it left the U.S. as the *only* industrialized nation not to mandate *paid* leave for mothers of newborns. As of 2015 we are still waiting for legislation to pass requiring *paid* leave. No wonder many women still choose not to return to work when their children are born! This is widespread knowledge yet our legislators have not seen fit to do anything about bringing the United States up to the standards of most every other country worldwide and we don't seem to have formed a groundswell of concern to press for movement on this yet! This I cannot explain.

Let's note, however, that some companies choose to tackle this on their own. Providing paid leave can make a huge difference as forward-thinking Google, Inc. has found. "Google was losing women after they had babies. The attrition rate for postpartum women was twice that for other employees. In response, Google lengthened maternity leave to five months from three and changed it from partial pay to full pay. Attrition decreased by 50 percent." (Miller, Claire Cain. "In Google's Inner Circle, a Falling Number of Women." New York Times. August 22, 2012. Accessed May 2015. (http://www.nytimes.com/2012/08/23/technology/in-googles-inner-circle-a-falling-number-of-women.html?pagewanted=all&_r=1).

"Vodafone, the telecommunications giant, recently announced in March that it was changing its global policies for new mothers. Now, all women will be offered 16 weeks of paid maternity leave and the ability to work a 30-hour week at full pay for six months after they return. Vodafone made this policy change after it found that 65 percent of the women who left the company following a maternity leave did so within their first year back. The company believes it will retain more talent and grow careers by instituting automatic flexibility for all new mothers." Heffernan, Lisa Endlich. "In Defense of the Mommy Track. MSN Money. May 4, 2015. (http://www.msn.com/en-us/money/careersandeducation/in-defense-of-the-mommy-track/ar-BBj98a9). This is great progress, but we need more companies like Google and Vodafone!

So here's what we are doing at my company. We are proactively in the process of developing a family-friendly leave policy stating that if an employee is full time, it will be her option to come back as a part-time employee after maternity leave. I'm motivated and influenced to provide this as I've known an IBM engineer who was terminated because she wouldn't come back full time once she had her first baby. Our policy will also address "flex time." As long as our clients are able to reach our engineers and trainers during business hours (regardless of the time zone they are in) then we'll provide our employees flex time to help them manage their work schedules so they can participate in their children's lives. In our organization we have a level of trust in our employees and believe that maternity/paternity leave or time off shouldn't have to adhere a limited number of days. Paid leave will be provided to valued members of our team who we wouldn't want to lose for this or any other reason. When you become a parent, everything changes in your life. Your employment agreement should follow suit.

It would be nice to fix the world's problems on your own and level that playing field once and for all, wouldn't it? In the meantime, here is what you can do now: Fix your own little corner of your business world first. Once you do this you can take on the bigger challenges working on them within corporate America.

Here are a few strategies to get yourself out there and in place early and effectively to ensure that you are on the right leadership path while letting everyone else know it:

- **Start where you are.** Statistics can be sobering. Facts can be daunting. Analyses can be challenging, particularly when so little seems to have changed for women in the workplace in the last few decades. While *knowledge* is critical, *action* is key to your success. If you want to have more success in your career and, ultimately, assume a leadership in your position or elsewhere, start where you are. Recognize, understand and sympathize with the national and even global plight of women in the workforce and then commit to doing something about it, starting with yourself.

- **Fill in the puzzle.** We all have gaps in our knowledge, in the skills we need to advance and even some of the personal skills we need to assume leadership. Make it part of your ongoing journey to fill in those gaps by completing the "leadership puzzle," one piece at a time. Take a class, earn a technical or a management certification. Attend a weekend seminar, find a mentor or sponsor. Make it your life's mission to be the most complete professional you know you can be.

- **Brag like a man.** As my father, who is an amazing trumpet player says, "Blow your own horn." If you want more recognition of your skill sets, accomplishments and effectiveness, take at least one cue from men and brag as they do. Learn to let others know, in whatever way you feel comfortable, what you're doing, how you're doing it and even how well you're doing it. One complaint I hear from women all the time is that no one notices their accomplishments, let alone rewards them. If that sounds familiar, let others know and perhaps you'll get the recognition you'll deserve. How will anyone recognize your greatness if they don't know what you do?

- **Be a marathoner, not a sprinter.** One of the biggest disservices a woman can do to herself is to grow impatient or rush success. Change—be it globally, nationally or in your company career path—takes time. Successful careers are a combination of life and work experiences that ultimately culminate in an achieved goal. Oftentimes, that goal can only be reached through a series of events that transpire over time. Someone has to move out of a leadership position to make room for you, and that won't always happen on your timeline. Perhaps you can propose and entirely new leadership position that doesn't exist, one that you have the perfect skills for? Don't wait forever, but don't jump ship with the goal in view just because it hasn't happened yet! Don't give up and don't get distracted. Stay the course.

- **The more the merrier.** Finally, don't go it alone. Whether socially or professionally, find a like-minded group of women to lean-in with, learn from or simply spend time with. You can schedule an after-hours get together with a group of women to vent in frustration with or to celebrate in accomplishment with. We all need friends and nowhere is this truer than for women in the workplace. These are the women who share many of your same interests and stresses. You can create a group of women who can count on each other help to bring each other up. Just as it says in Proverbs, "iron sharpens iron." Put another way, "You can always tell the strong women, they are the one's building each other up instead of tearing each other down," a widely circulated quote on Facebook, Twitter and Instagram.

- **Don't be afraid to ask for accommodation as a working parent.** Once you have proven yourself in your workplace, you should be able to ask for occasional accommodations of your needs as a parent; starting or leaving early sometimes or working from home. I can't speak for every employer but I can say that *as* an employer, I would rather have a frank discussion with a great employee of what we can do to meet her needs instead of losing a good employee when there might have been a way to save the engagement.

True change will occur when others recognize your potential and the potential of women in general and respond accordingly. By putting some of the above "best practices" into action, however, you can avoid becoming part of the problem, and start working toward the solutions we all need. Vow to be 100% invested in yourself and your career and take it as far as you can with your talents and your commitment. Be fair to yourself and to the women your work with, to the benefit of all.

Field Notes

My first full-time office manager, Karen, had twin, five-year old girls. She was diligent about making sure they were silent whenever they were around. It was lost on me at the time just how significant this was to keep children that age silent because I didn't have children then.

Karen was my first employee who needed to start early so she could tend to "kid stuff." Sometimes she asked to take time off from her job to accommodate some need of her twins. Fortunately, these requests came at a good time when our company was past a big growth period and we could create a more flexible team meeting schedule to be sensitive to Karen's needs.

When I became a mother myself, with my first daughter and then my second, I managed to take only 30 days off from work. I was able to get back to work quickly because I found a way to work at home. Thus began my "new work schedule" which I still basically follow today. When I need to put in more than 40 hours during a work week, which I frequently do, I use the hours after my daughters have gone to sleep. I've also found ways to work on weekends while the girls and I are out; while watching sports, taking them to bouncy house, or zoo rides. Sometimes I need to get very creative.

The one thing I strictly enforce is that no one will ever hear my children in the background while I am on a conference call or when I telecommute from a home office. I've made it a point to never let my clients know when I am not "in" the office. This began a while back when telecommuting wasn't as widely spread/accepted as it is now. I strongly feel that your environment should not negatively impact or influence your participation in business.

My company, ECS, does maintain an office but thankfully we now live in a connected world now and business often gets carried on regardless of the participant's locations. If technology has done anything for women it is this, it has given many of us the ability to work, at least part of the time, in greater proximity to our children and our company policies take advantage of these advancements. Even if we have hired someone to bear the full-time responsibility of caring for our children, it's a great leap forward to be able to choose to work from home near a sick child or to extend that option to another working mom when it's needed.

The Takeaway

You would think that, in this day and age, writing about how women are underrepresented—and underutilized—in business would be passé. But as the facts clearly indicate, women still represent *less* than one-third of corporate board positions and that number has been holding steady for far too long. Hopefully I've challenged not only your notions of the broader problem at large, but also given you some practical advice on how to rectify it, one step at a time. It's important to look at the challenges we face in business with an eye to finding the grey areas and to creating more of them. Business and family life are *not* antithetical to each other and it doesn't have to be an all or nothing prospect. We may never hit a perfect balance but we can meet somewhere in the middle. Now let's look at how women and men differ in business and why that's not always a bad thing.

THE DIFFERENCE BETWEEN FEMALE AND MALE MANAGERS: WOMEN'S SUPERIOR SOFT SKILLS

"Tis skill, not strength, that governs a ship."
—**Thomas Fuller**

W omen bring uniquely feminine qualities and abilities to the workplace. Women who have smashed through the glass ceiling have done it because they have learned how to emphasize their femininity, not in spite of it. Our instincts and emotional intelligence can be a great bonus when we learn how to use them successfully in business. For example, often, female leaders can more readily manage crisis using the feminine "superpowers," those womanly traits that are commonly referred to as "Soft Skills."

Soft Skills are typically defined as; listening, adaptability, good judgment, communication, positivity and integrity. Historically hard "masculine" skills have been seen as the embodiment of successful leadership. Most can envision the brash, take-no-prisoners, dictatorial style of the archaic, tyrannical male boss. This is the long running stereotype of the "Man in control," the "Barking Boss." They're great caricatures to laugh at in movies but who really wants to work for one? The truth is nobody does. Thankfully, things have changed and perhaps have even been influenced by the greater influx of women into the workforce over time.

When we first began to tap at the glass ceiling, many of us women climbing the corporate ladder erroneously thought that the way to get to the top was to act—and in some cases even dress—like a man. I can still remember a fashion trend in the 1980's and 90's when women wore suits with big shoulder pads and neckties. I hate to admit I was one of those women. I had more than a few of those types of suits. That's old thinking now and as women have gained their small but firm foothold in Corporate America, the dress fabrics and the management styles available to women have softened.

One emerging management trend is called "Transformational Leadership," where managers guide change through inspiration and connection. They seek to build trust and confidence by empowering subordinates to develop their potential. Many studies suggest that women are more transformational in style than men. Such leadership models are inclusive and collaborative—exactly the strengths associated with women. (Key, Mary, PhD. CEO Road Rules: Right Focus, Right People, Right Execution. Nicholas Brealey Publishing, September 12, 2006.)

Women have proven that they are capable and substantive and, as a result, they are freer to employ their "softer" but equally powerful skills, such as empathy and active listening. Soft doesn't have to mean ineffective. Many of us are not even aware of this advantage that we have. We have misinterpreted "soft" as weak. Nothing could be further from the truth. Managing like a tyrant is the fastest way to alienate your employees.

There are many areas of management where you can directly apply strong soft skills. For example: coaching, empowering employees, encouraging teamwork, sharing information and designating responsibility in a consultative rather than dictatorial manner. If you know that you are weak in this area, countless soft skills training courses are available. Invest in one.

How to use Soft Skills to Your Advantage

Countless studies and articles now support the notion that female managers make great bosses. Female managers are more likely to monitor employee feedback and development more closely, promote interpersonal communication and include employees in the decision-making process.

No matter what your first impressions are about soft versus hard management, the proof is in the pudding, so to speak. Women really do make great leaders. You can feel confident that there is nothing in your femininity that will prevent you from ascending to a spot in top management. Nothing.

Sure, you may still have to weather the occasional gender stereotyping—such as the ideas that women are less invested and somehow weaker—but you can prove the stereotypes wrong with your hard work and dedication. Stereotyping is a holdover from an archaic view of corporate culture and such ideas as these can weaken companies today.

Here are some guidelines you will want to follow to assist you in establishing your soft powers:

- **Remain Authentic**. Be true to yourself and stay confident in who you are. The day will come when you understand that the truth really does always come out. Maintain your ethics, honesty and frankness. Wear a soft dress but wear it over a tough heart and mind. After all, how inauthentic is it to see a woman marching around in a suit and tie, trying to act just like a man?

- **Remain Flexible**. Keep your leadership style adaptable to the situations as they develop and not engraved in stone. Always be ready to change your management style as needed in different situations. Play up your feminine traits when it's appropriate to achieve your company's objectives and tone them down when it isn't.

- **Create a supportive network**. The old adage, "To make a friend you have to be a friend" also holds true in business. As a woman in leadership, extending yourself in friendship appropriately builds trust. You won't compromise your position as a superior by befriending your staff as long as you keep it professional. I'm not talking about hanging out with employees at happy hour but about being genuinely interested in their lives and their families.

When you are getting to know your co-workers, don't delve but inquire. Everyone deserves a degree of privacy and managers don't need to know every detail about an employee's life. But if you know just enough and genuinely care about what's going on with your co-workers outside the office, you can more easily manage if their work falls off. Do this and you will always know when to offer your empathy and understanding to support them to get back on track. If employees and co-workers feel that you value them, they'll shoot for the moon for you.

Field Notes

In my company real life, collaborative management means that my management teams and I repeat the following phrase often, "We don't care HOW a task is completed we care THAT it is completed." This creates an openness to collaborate on better and different ways to accomplish tasks within our entire team. In the process of allowing members of the team to accomplish their goals in the way they see fit, they often have come up with better ways that were never tried before and that we might not have discovered. This openness allows ideas and practices to develop organically. I can tell you as well, that when ideas flow up as often as they flow down, everyone feels truly invested. To me, that's collaborative management at its best.

The Takeaway

It's important to realize that as a woman in business, you bring to the table feminine traits and characteristics that men do not. This is actually a strength, not a deficiency. You may look around and see that management and leadership is dominated by men, but that doesn't mean that your aspirations to management require you to behave like men in business. In fact, it's quite the opposite. The female tendency to nurture the best from everyone and the ability to include everyone to build consensus and encourage collaboration are some of the feminine abilities and characteristics you want to maximize, not suppress. Studies back up the notion that women really do make great leaders so you shouldn't feel disadvantaged.

When I started this chapter I thought it was important to recognize the strengths women have over men. It might seem odd but this was something I didn't realize until later in my career. I wonder if some of the reason for his was that I never thought of my management style being different from men. I think this type of thinking contributed to my belief that nothing could hold me back just because I was a young woman. This was due, in part, to having parents who never allowed to me to think that I was limited because I was a girl.

Furthermore, and it relates to my upbringing of my daughters, I pay special attention not to limit the toys they play with based on their gender. It's always bothered me very much whenever I've observed mothers saying "this is a girls toy" or "this is a boys toy" to their children. I'm diligently making sure that my daughters understand, no toys are off limits to them. Yes, there are differences between boys and girls and there are differences in the management styles of men and women. It's great to observe and understand this but sometimes it's also important to refuse to burden yourself with gender based limitations and pre-conceived notions in order to become the best manager you can be.

WOMEN'S WEAKNESS—
EMOTIONALITY THE
DOUBLE-EDGED SWORD

Your intellect may be confused, but your emotions will never lie to you."

—Roger Ebert

A fter all this talk of the appropriate use of our femininity and soft skills, it's time to take a closer look at ourselves. We women are emotional creatures. We can't help it. We're literally—and genetically—hardwired to be this way. According to Dr. Peggy Drexler, in her article "Emotions and Work" for HuffingtonPost.com, "Women have six times more prolactin—the tear hormone—than men. Plus, women have larger tear ducts, which may account for why women gush and men trickle." (Drexler, Peggy, PhD. "Emotions and Work." The Huffington Post. June 29, 2013. Accessed February, 2015. http://www.huffingtonpost.com/peggydrexler/emotions-and-work_b_3521661.html). Just because we're scientifically wired to be more emotional doesn't mean that we can or should be crying in the workplace. Losing control of your emotions the workplace is usually inappropriate. Don't despair. I'm going to teach you how to manage this.

For Crying Out Loud—There is No Crying in Corporate America. Is there?

Before moving forward, let me make a quick disclaimer: This is not *me* telling you to ignore your emotions, dampen your instincts or deny those feelings that make you unique, individual and valuable to everyone in the company in the first place. In fact your uniqueness, your passions and your ability to *feel* are what fuel your leadership potential. After all, who wants an emotionless, "cookie cutter," play-by-the-rulebook leader? What I'm talking about is learning to control those emotions appropriately in business and making sure to avoid managing yourself or others by your emotions. I'm going to give you a technique for how to do this.

First, to emphasize how a big of a challenge this has proven to be for some, let me share with you that according to recent studies, as many as one in four women in the workforce is now using a psychotropic prescription drug (an antidepressant or anti-anxiety) to control her emotions at her workplace.

Kelly Wallace of CNN reports on Doctor of Psychopharmacology and Psychiatry Julie Holland, MD's book "Moody Bitches." Quoting Holland, "Women have this idea that we are supposed to not be moody and we're supposed to tamp down that moodiness…It's like a problem to be fixed and really, I think it's our greatest asset. It's certainly our greatest psychological asset. After all, our empathetic nature helps us understand nonverbal babies—and not-always-the-most-communicative husbands and business partners…So, why on earth have all of those qualities come to be viewed as a source of weakness, not strength?"

Wallace's CNN report also says that according to Holland's patients, often, such medications don't always work! Holland describes a patient who called her up in tears and asked for a new antidepressants because the ones she was taking weren't preventing her from crying at work. When Holland asked her what caused her to cry, she said her boss was being difficult. Holland responded that "What was needed was a plan to confront her boss, not a prescription for a new medication!" (Wallace, Kelly. "Why women are medicating away their moodiness." CNN. March 6, 2015. Accessed March 31, 2105).

The issue is not women's emotions. It is the perception, or stereotype, of the "hysterical irrational, out of control, hormonal, crying woman." Women seem to fear this as much as men do. Are you thinking that these stereotypes don't exist anymore? Think again. Consider what this CEO of a marketing company in Texas had to say about Hillary Clinton's bid for the 2016 presidency.

"With the hormones we have, there is no way [a woman] should be able to start a war," she wrote in her post, per KTVT, Texas. "Yes I run my own business and I love it and I am great at it BUT that is not the same as being the President that should be left to a man, a good, strong, honorable man." (Mosbergen, Dominique. "Female CEO Says Women 'Shouldn't Be President' Because Of 'Different Hormones,' 'Biblical Reasoning'." The Huffington Post, Accessed April 15, 2015. http://www. huffingtonpost.com/2015/04/15/ceo-women-shouldnt-be-president-cheryl-rios_n_7067564.html)

Yes, these stereotypes do exist and surprisingly, men aren't the only ones perpetuating them! In this instance, this CEO received a lot of backlash from women, and men, around the *world* for making such ridiculous and untrue statements. Certainly, as Margaret Thatcher, Indira Gandhi and many other leaders of countries who just happen to have been women have demonstrated, there is not a single role a woman isn't suited for on the strict basis of her gender. Not one!

Permission to Take 10... or More

So let me offer you this. One of my earliest mentors, Robyn Button, taught me a simple but invaluable technique: walk away whenever you begin to feel too emotional in a business situation. It was Robyn who let me know that I could give myself permission to just excuse myself and take a breather. Often, a walk outside the building, a lunch break away from my desk or taking a drive somewhere alone was enough for me to vent my feelings in private without fear of embarrassment or regret. Then, when I was ready I could go back to face whatever the situation was with my emotions diffused and fresh perspective.

Sometimes in order to do that I needed to pretend that I didn't have a personal stake involved, which wasn't always easy. In fact, I also learned from Robyn never, never make the mistake of making any major decisions based on emotions. Let the emotion out of the equation and then you can look at the pros and the cons of the decision in true balance.

Here was one of those invaluable times when I was very fortunate to have a great female mentor who'd share this kind of advice with me. I probably would not have figured it out so quickly on my own. Now, I'm always sure to share this concept whenever I can with the women who work for me. This technique works! Emotions pass and with a little space you can get back to business. It's empowering to learn to manage your emotion without needing to deny—or medicate—them!

If we consider where the notion of women's emotional weakness comes from, it is this, right or wrongly, that women occasionally cry in the workplace and that is, rightly or wrongly, enough to be seen as weak. Men express their emotionality by yelling and that is seen as being powerful. That's not to say that yelling doesn't have a negative impact, but it isn't seen as being weak. In business everyone strives to maintain the "power position."

It isn't fair but this is an area women have to work hard at developing an alternative reaction when the heat is on because if *we* blow our stacks, we're seen as irrational and if we cry we're seen as weak. Our true strength rests in learning to manage ourselves so that we don't do either of these but instead find alternative means of expressing our feelings in a socially appropriate way at the office.

So here is the Flip Side: Emotions Can Work in Your Favor

The irony is that in spite of all my cautioning and in spite of any preconceptions you may have, as author Julie Holland pointed out, in certain circumstances your emotions can still be your ally. *Feelings* can help you slow down long enough to deeply consider all your options and that can help you make good decisions. *Emotions* can provide you with intuition and hunches and those are things you can act on. Your emotions provide your unique perspective. Just remember emotions can also get in the way of your reason and cause you to respond with your heart instead of your head when the latter is required. There is a time for emotions and a time for intellect. Learning to manage both will benefit you tremendously in business.

So the bottom line is while emotions can be positive, managing other people and projects strictly by emotional reaction is a bad idea because it will invariably cause you to lose the respect of your colleagues. Our workplaces aren't our homes, our hangouts or our emotional playgrounds. The office is not a group therapy sessions where it is important for us to let everyone know all about our feelings. Business is business. Here are a few guidelines to follow to help you discern where the line of appropriate emotionality in the workplace falls.

Key Points for Managing your Emotions:

- **Don't set yourself up to fail.** Success in business requires you to maintain a clear head to perform at peak efficiency. Managing through mood swings, temper tantrums, ego or other emotions will make your leadership, and your performance, sporadic and unreliable.

- **Respect is earned not given.** Just because you've achieved a position as a team leader, department manager or CEO doesn't mean people will automatically respect you. Awards, bonuses and promotions are tied closely to respect. Don't be the micromanager who thrives on keeping employees on their toes with threatening behavior so they never know when the next emotional outburst or tirade is coming. One of the fastest ways to lose respect is by leading emotionally with no rhyme or reason to your actions. Lead like this and you'll leave a trail of hurt feelings and wake of unwise decisions. Trust me: you won't be in management long.

- **Learn to love facts and ideas.** Businesses run on facts, ideas, strategies and plans. Financial reports, profits and losses (P&L's), debt to income ratios, performance reviews, statistics, proformas, schemas… these are the lifeblood of business. Focus on these and your opinion will be respected in the organization. As Eleanor Roosevelt said: "Great minds discuss ideas, average minds discuss events, and small minds discuss people." (This is actually a quote I love and I try to bring it into conversations often when I find a conversation needs to be turned around).

- **Never let them see you sweat.** A famous advertisement for "Dry Idea" antiperspirant that ran in the 1980's, the same decade that produced the movie "Working Girl," caught lots of attention with the slogan, "Never Let Them See You Sweat." It was good advice. Stock up on your own "emotional antiperspirant" and keep yourself in check. Losing control of your emotions in the 21st Century will land you as much trouble now as back then. You want to always appear confident.

- **Own any temporary insanity.** Finally, if you do let your emotions get too out of control and all your self-management tools fly out the window, own it! We've all lost control and said things we haven't necessarily meant at some point. If it happens, issue unreserved apologies as soon as your reason returns, even if you aren't completely to blame. In business you don't ever want the *last* impression you leave to be a bad one. If you screw up in business, just own it and fix it. We all make mistakes. The key is to own your mistakes when you make them. People will forget your mistakes but they'll remember your accountability, and that will gain you respect.

Field Notes

Once we were on an installation at the large corporate headquarters site of a company located in the Pacific Northwest. It was under new construction and the air conditioning for the server room wasn't installed yet. The project manager decided that our engineering team would begin work anyway. This was the wrong decision and my team should not have begun until these environmental controls were installed and tested. As a result our team was working in 90 degrees and things were not good for us or for the hardware we were working on. Instead of handing this, the project manager lost it and he basically checked out and wouldn't return calls to our team members or the client. Needless to say that was the beginning of the end of his career.

Another time, I showed up to assist in the migration cutover for Coca Cola on the East Coast. The project manager on this job was clearly over his head with the direction of this particular migration. I was told there was lack of sleep involved but this Project Manager became abusive and in appropriate in nature to the project team, in effect "losing it" before all of us due to the pressure he was under. Too bad this person didn't know enough to step out of the situation entirely and "calm down." His lack of ability to manage himself made for a very uncomfortable situation for all of us in and created a very unhappy client.

The Takeaway

The best way to handle yourself emotionally at the office is to make sure you take the time to envision a plan beforehand of *exactly* what you will do in different sticky situations and scenarios and then practice your responses before you actually need them. Develop your offense so you don't need a defense. As in most other crisis, emotional ones are more easily avoided when you're thoroughly prepared to handle them. When it gets to be too much to handle, excuse yourself and return when you are composed.

Emotions pass, so don't let them get out of control. If a situation is really bad, then address the issues with the powers that be when you are rational, not when you are being emotionally reactive. Don't snuff your potential with a snap decision or an emotional explosion. If you need to leave a job, do it rationally with forethought and by following the procedures set in place so you don't burn your bridges.

THE DOUBLE WHAMMY OF
BEING YOUNG AND FEMALE

"Every girl should use what Mother Nature gave her before Father Time takes it away."
—Dr. Laurence J. Peter

Youth is fantastic. This is probably something almost everyone agrees with. Youth in business can be one of the most positive attributes anyone can bring to their career. Young workers bring a positive, unjaded attitude and an eagerness to find solutions while people who've been in the workforce for a while tend to focus more on established processes and the way things have always been done. Youth brings enthusiasm, innovation and creativity. Every employee wants to be noticed and recognized for their contributions. With youth, however, this poses a particular challenge.

The challenge is that first and foremost in corporate America you are often only as good as your *last* project, your last win or your last accomplishment. When you are young you have no "last" anything. You're a blank slate without a track record and people who are key to your success have nothing to base their expectations of you on.

What I found in my own experience was that when I was just starting out as a young, female college grad, my voice wasn't given much weight or credibility. This was something I wanted to change but I had no idea how to go about it.

Women Making Inroads

"It's time to smash every last glass ceiling."
—Hillary Clinton

In some organizations the management structure has been in place for decades and this can create even more of a barrier to youth. This barrier may seem impossible to overcome because the "gatekeepers" are overprotective and suspicious of all things new, which includes you as a bright, young executive. Even more so if you are female.

Early in my career, I made a very memorable "youthful" mistake. In this situation, I was the engineer on a project to upgrade a number of retail sites that were spread across the country in six states! About a third of the way into the project, I needed to engage with a technician who was also very young. He thought his ideas on how the project should be run were the "best" ideas. Well, I thought my ideas were the best. After all, I had completed site-survey preparations and I had established processes and procedures to insure our success, the project had already established success, yet he would have no part of my directing him.

Being the youthful, enthusiastic woman I was, I was quick to let him know that *our* way—*my* way—was the *only* way to implement, and that he needed to follow *my* management. Needless to say, we did not hit it off. We both suffered through the project. When it was completed, I chalked it all up to experience and brushed it off at the time even telling myself that this conflict didn't matter as I would *never* work with this technician in the future. Famous last words, as the saying goes.

Fate, it seems, was not content to leave things at that and less than 10 years later, that very technician was *the* Portland branch manager for our client, Siemens. There I was sitting in his office after we'd lost nearly *all* our new business in Oregon. I was literally begging for him to engage our team.

After all, it was so long ago when we'd butted heads, would he even remember?

Well of course he did! We did not secure any projects in Oregon during his tenure. Youthful lesson learned, the hard way! The other lesson here is to remember to always keep your "nose clean" in your industry with everyone you have the opportunity to work with. You never know what life change may affect your career. With this recession economy we've learned that what was up is down and down is up. Know also that experts in any given industry are recycled and it's never wise to burn bridges or make foes.

Why a Degree is not Enough

> "A young woman stepped out into the courtyard with a bright smile and a fresh perspective. She wore a crisp, black gown and a mortar board clipped firmly to her hair with bobby pins. Graduation day, the culmination of all her efforts, was finally here. The sheepskin she'd be handed later that day sealed her fate as a woman with infinite choices."
>
> **—Francesca Kennedy**

I was that woman. When I was young in the workplace, degree in hand along with a new business suit and a designer briefcase, I felt I was ready to take on the world. I thought I had everything I'd need. In some ways I did have everything—as much as we all do—but in many practical ways, I did not. What I was not armed with—and what they could not pack into my degree—was an understanding of the importance of *organizational dynamics*, something that is learned by observation and takes time to assess and evaluate. When you are very young (or starting again in a new industry) it is wise to realize that you bring to the table your current knowledge, but very little direct experience.

So, if you approach business challenges based solely on your knowledge, especially when you are working with people who have a lot more experience, you won't be successful. That's why mentors and relationships can be so useful, however they take time to nurture. It's imperative that you take advantage of the knowledge and experience of others. Using the knowledge of others is also the shortest distance between A and B sometimes in not having to learn from your own mistakes.

In my experience being young can also cause you to be shortsighted. What I mean is that in our youth we are looking forward, but not very far forward. The "long term" for someone in their 20's might translate to five to 10 years of time. Where the long term for an older employee may foresee today through retirement. This type of shortsightedness can hinder you as a young businessperson. I certainly found that out the hard way. I found that focusing on the short term, things such as immediate monetary benefits or lofty titles could end up being harmful. How? If you are only looking at what benefits you today, you may take career positions offered to you that might not be in your strategic interest long term. So set your scope a little further out. Let your minimum short term career goals be looking forward 15 years.

Field Notes

My company once landed a contract for the FBI in San Diego. At the time, I had a couple of new college graduates, myself and another junior engineer along on the project. We were all young and attractive ranging from our early twenties to mid-thirties. Well, the FBI put my team in the basement level of their building right outside the telephone closet in the hall. Because there were security issues they were concerned with us accessing their system through modems, our usual method, so we had to be hard-wired and close by.

So here we were, young engineers all hardwired to their new phone system, programming, all in business suits, and everyone under 35. The hall we were tucked away in also lead directly to the lunchroom. As the FBI agents made their visits to the lunch room that day, the word began to spread quickly that a bunch of young females were working in the basement...

or so my customer told me. Suddenly it seemed like every agent in the building had left his desk and headed to the lunchroom with a sudden need for snacks!

At one point during the course of the contract, according to my client, they just had to tell some of the agents to stop going to the lunchroom. Truthfully, it got a little distracting for everyone. My team was also getting a little excited about all those good looking FBI agents! It may have seemed harmless enough but we maintain a strict "no fraternizing with the client" policy within our company. It's well spelled out in the employee handbook. The work is just too important and we have to maintain our policy to be taken seriously and get the job done. This sort of challenge likely would never had happened if we were a group of middle-aged men. Luckily, even though we were young we all knew our policies and we remained professional at all times.

In another instance, I had an excellent trainer named "Deborah" on staff who was quite petite and very attractive. I have to say she looked quite a bit younger than her 25 years. Despite her misleading appearance, I knew she was an awesome trainer so when I got a call from a client saying that Deborah seemed to be more concerned about her looks than she was about the class she was instructing, I suspected the issue might be jealousy. It had to be, as Deborah was a seasoned and experienced trainer!

When I spoke to Deborah about the complaint and asked her why she thought it was called in, she said there was a group of gals about her age in the class and that they were giving her the once over—along with a bit of attitude. After class they were talking about her when, unbeknownst to them, she was in the bathroom listening. Here she was, a great trainer but they just could not get over her youth and appearance! In this case there was nothing she ought to have done differently, it was just her youth working against her as it can sometimes. I think in addition to jealously—this speaks to the idea that sometimes when you are really good at what you do, people will look for something else they can criticize. Often it's frivolous. I've had this happen to me quite a few times in my career.

As strange as this may sound, I once had a vendor complain that my company and I were "too positive" and "too optimistic." I laughed about this of course, knowing that since it probably meant he could find nothing substantive to complain about and this was the best he could do. In my company, our optimism stems from our confidence in our ability and also from our experience. In this case experience allowed us to foresee things coming together as they should, even in the midst of the project having the appearance of going astray, so to speak. This client has since changed his tune as our work result for his project proved to merit our optimism. When we know we can do the work, there's no reason to ever be anything but optimistic.

The Takeaway

There are many positive associations with youth in business. New blood, fresh perspective and enthusiasm are great qualities found in young employees. The main challenge, however is lack of experience. When you are young in your career sometimes you'll need to observe more than you venture to offer while still finding a way to develop your voice and have it heard. Objections and criticisms of your "greenness" will be just that and in time you will have the all experience you need. So defer to those with more experience for a while, learn from them and bide your time. No one stays green forever and it won't be long before there's a newer kid than you and you are the experienced one.

LISTEN MORE, TALK LESS.
THE MAGIC OF ACTIVE LISTENING

"The most courageous act is still to think for yourself. Aloud."
—Coco Chanel

L uckily, great female leaders tend to be good listeners and every good listener knows the cardinal rule is to speak *less* and pay attention *more*, often asking questions and repeating back what you have heard for clarification. This also confirms to the speaker that you have heard correctly what was said and you understand. Effective listening is a helpful tool for resolving conflicts, building trust, inspiring people and developing strong teams.

As the head of the team you are supposed to know what employees are thinking about, what issues they're dealing with and how to help them. The only way to achieve this is to listen. But it just isn't all about being quiet and paying attention. It's also important to be aware of body language, facial expressions and mood. If you work life presents you the opportunity to be part of a project team, this is a great opportunity to practice your listening skills. As a team member you can sit back and listen and watch as each member speaks. This is something I like to do with new clients so I can observe their culture and it helps me understand if they have the listening skills successful for efforts.

As the head of a team: Speaking less and listening more has many benefits. Active listening offers the opportunity to think before speaking, to take in what the employee is saying and to respond accordingly. Active listening also gives you more time to process what the other person is talking about. This includes analyzing not just what but also how something has been said. Paying attention to the way an employee is speaking may be essential for discovering an underlying issue you might otherwise miss.

Listening intently will provide you the time to process and consider all the information surrounding an issue before making any decisions. With the right information, when it's time for your input you will be able to choose your words carefully and make yourself as clear as possible, leaving no room for confusion.

Once you've met someone who truly practices active and intent listening you'll know the difference. I've been fortunate to share a lunch with John Boas, CEO, and Founder of San Francisco Honda. I've never met anyone who comes close to displaying the level of intense listening of Mr. Boas. His body language and intent eye focus is unique. For all intents and purposes when you are talking to him, he makes you feel that what you have to say is the absolutely, most fascinating thing known to man. Certainly what I had to say that day was important but far from profound. Yet, I stepped away from that lunch with such an impression. That lunch was probably some ten years ago although I remember it and John like it was last Monday.

Here are some tips to improve your listening skills:

- **Listen to understand.** Simply hearing someone's words isn't enough. It is important to listen for meaning. After understanding an issue, then you can respond.
- **Be still and quiet.** This way you will have the opportunity to hear the words, along with the tone, and the meaning and the body language behind the words.

- **Don't interrupt the speaker.** Don't interrupt your employees or clients while they are speaking. This one is very difficult at time for most people.
- **Keep eye contact.** By keeping eye contact you will pick up any expressions and notice when they don't match the words someone is saying. For example, you notice raised eyebrows and eyes looking away when someone is saying a project is going great. What might that tell you?
- **Ask questions.** Clarify and restate to make sure you understand.
- **Ask for feedback.** Great leaders with great listening skills solicit feedback and take action based on that feedback.
- **Never try to impress with your response.** If you are listening but working out your response at the same time, you aren't actively listening.

Now here are some interesting facts provided by The International Listening Association (www.listen.org):

- Most of us are distracted, preoccupied or forgetful about 75% of the time we should be listening.
- We listen at 125-250 words per minute, but think at 1000-3000 words per minute.

- Just after we listen to someone, we only recall about 50% of what they said.
- Long-term, we only remember 20% of what we hear.
- More than 35 business studies indicate that listening is a top skill needed for success in business.
- 85% of what we know we have learned through listening.
- Humans generally listen at a 25% comprehension rate.
- In a typical business day, we spend 45% of our time listening, 30% of our time talking, 16% reading and 9% writing.
- Less than 2% of all professionals have had formal education or learning to understand and improve listening skills and techniques.

The bottom line is that when it comes to working with others, particularly managing and guiding them, there is magic in skilled, active listening. It's magic that must be learned and practiced in order to be applied. Few of us are truly skilled at active listening. Our inability to harness this powerful tool can lead to misunderstanding, wasted time and in businesses that always translates to the bottom line by lowering productivity. Without understanding your employees you can't build an effective team. We'll look at that next.

Field Notes

If you work life presents you the opportunity to be part of a project team, this is a great opportunity to practice your listening skills. As a team member you can sit back and listen and watch as each member speaks. This is something I like to do with new clients so I can observe their culture. It helps me understand if they have the listening skills to be successful in their efforts.

The Takeaway

The first requirement of participating with a coworker, client or on a team is to listen. Active listening is a skill that must be learned and practiced. Few people know what it is to really listen. We talked about what exactly is required and why great listening skills are crucial to being an effective manager.

CORPORATIONS ARE TEAMS

"It is amazing how much people can get done if they do not worry about who gets the credit."
—Sandra Swinger

We are all reaching for success in our careers. The good news is that corporate America is actually structured and delineated to help insure *everyone's* success. Corporations are structured to insure productivity. From the outside, it might look like corporations celebrate strong leaders and fiercely independent individuals above everyone else, but that isn't necessarily the case. It's hard to imagine Living Omnimedia without Martha Stewart, the OWN Network without Oprah, Facebook without Mark Zuckerberg or Apple without Steve Jobs. However, those very same leaders would go to great lengths to say that they are just the "tip of the spear."

In other words, behind every great leader is an even greater team. Those who ultimately became great leaders know that being an amazing team member along the way helped them to become the great leader they are today. So if leading is your ultimate goal, step back, take a breather and learn how to look at the whole playing field and everyone on it.

Playing Well With Others, the Importance of Team Sports

Fair warning, this is NOT about how to throw a softball, slam-dunk a basketball or kick a field goal. It is about the benefits and importance of participating in team sports. So why, you may ask, are team sports so important? I'm glad you asked! I almost don't know where to begin. Team sports can be useful in so many ways by helping you learn how to be a valued *member* of something bigger than yourself.

One definition of the word corporation, according to Webster's, is "of, relating to, or formed into a unified body of individuals." Just as your hand doesn't act without the involvement of your arm, shoulder and brain, a corporation acts with the involvement of all its members as well. If you have always played alone, you'll have a tougher time understanding that concept.

What You Learn By Playing Team Sports:

- **How to play well with others.** Team sports are all about playing well with others, and in case you haven't noticed… so is the business world. Companies, like teams, hire all sorts of people with all sorts of strengths, and weaknesses and potentials. You can't just "play" with the ones like you. You have to work well with everyone on the team if you ever hope to lead them. You also learn that sometimes no matter whether or not you get along with all your fellow team members it takes all of you to accomplish your goals so you must learn to operate as a cohesive unit.

- **How to learn by doing.** A good coach will provide the opportunity for you to play almost every position on the team so you can discover where you fit best, be that as a kicker, quarterback or defensive lineman. Often we think we're one thing when we're actually quite another. Team sports allow us to find our own way while still contributing to the team as a whole.

- **How to respect authority.** If you want to earn respect, you must give respect. This is true if you're leading a team or a company. Respect that each team member has a specific role and unique talents. Respecting what everyone brings to the table will assist you in engendering respect back toward yourself and as leader you must command respect.

- **You are only as strong as your weakest player.** If you understand this, you will "rally" in way to assist that player knowing the good will benefit the entire team.

TIME OUT! Let's take a second to consider how to *command* respect. "The only way to command respect from others is not to *demand* it. Leaders who are admired and respected have *earned* that admiration and respect. Respect is given to others only when they are deemed worthy of receiving the honor. This is the same for sports, whereby the MVP of the game was awarded based on skill and achievement within the game and then the immediate respect for that title comes after.

On a technical implementation team, each job is entirely dependent on the others. For instance, if the software engineer doesn't upgrade the software version and apply all the patches necessary, the database engineer can't upload the database. If the client doesn't ready the network for suitability when the VOIP implementation takes place, the calls won't process. If one team member doesn't do their job completely, the other team members will fail. In our very real practical experience, if the project manager doesn't make sure all the tasks are complete, all sides of the project are a complete nightmare. This absence of coordination and cooperation may result in cost overruns and delays in scheduling.

As you can see, this is why team sports are about so much more than just throwing a ball or making a basket. Unlike individual sports such as downhill skiing or golfing, team sports rely on the strength of *every* team member working as a cohesive unit to produce the desired results. The stronger the team, the better those results.

Business is a team sport, because it is collaborative. A corporation is literally a "body" of individuals. You have your team leader, or the CEO, as the head, team captains, or the managers and supervisors are the hearts. Team players—the employees—are the vital organs and limbs, if you will. Working together, each team member plays a role. Knowing your role on a team is crucial to eventually becoming the team leader, or CEO, one day.

So let's look at what *makes* a great team player. Unfortunately, becoming a great team player isn't always as easy as just showing up and kicking the ball around. If you have never played on a team sport, now is the time. There are many post graduate leagues to just get out and play in, but for today, here's what it takes.

The Traits of a Great Team Player:

- **Enthusiasm.** A great team player is always enthusiastic. She's always up for a challenge, ready to greet the day, grab the team coffee, go the extra mile or help out whenever and wherever needed. She is enthusiastic about the team's goal. This is not the same as being an errand girl. It's all about supporting the team when needed in an enthusiastic, positive and helpful manner. Enthusiasm to do whatever is needed for the sake of the team.

- **Patience.** Everyone wants everything yesterday these days. We all want ways to skip the team player part, and get right to Most Valuable Player (MVP) status. Great team players understand that's not their role for today. They may aspire to becoming the MVP one day, but they know to accomplish this they must never forget that the goals of the *team* must always outweigh their goals as *individual* players.

- **Develop Passion.** Even when a project is something you're not passionate about—such as editing a technical brochure or putting together a quarterly budget report a great team player always finds something to *get* passionate about. Maybe it's who she is working with, maybe it's who the report is for, or maybe it's simply her goal of leading one day. She will find a way to get passionate about whatever she is working on, and that's what makes her a great team player indeed.

- **Curiosity.** Great team players want to know everything about everything. Who are their teammates? What is the coach like? Who are their opponents? What can we do to up our game? Uncovering the answers to these questions drives not only curiosity but also effectiveness, as team members gain proficiency and value for the team with each answer they seek.
- **Dedication.** Great team players show up at every practice, sometimes for additional practice, to put in the effort and get the work done. They're the first one in the office in the morning and the last one to leave at the end of the day.
- **Effectiveness.** You can be friendly, curious, passionate and all the rest but at the end of the day, you need to show results. Get busy or go home applies here.

Teams rely on great players to make them run. So do companies. As you progress on your team, keep something in mind: Always respect your team's leaders, even if your team leader, coach or MVP is slow, plodding, uninformed and ill-equipped to lead, recognize his or her authority and act accordingly. Businesses are hierarchies with a certain pecking order, and if you continually disrupt the natural flow or order by complaining about, undermining or disrespecting your boss, you won't just be hurting her but the entire organization. What kind of team player is that?

Being a great team player is about knowing your position and how to do it well. The fact is you can't always be the MVP. No matter how many trophies, awards or commendations you collect. Sometimes you just have to be the one to help lead your <u>team</u> to victory, and forget the idea of reaping all the rewards or the spotlight for yourself. When you come to terms with your own role in the organization, you'll be a great team player.

Field Notes

In the second year of the first company I started, I was always one of the first to come into my client's office and often I was the last one to leave. In fact one night I remember that the office cleaning staff accidentally tripped the security alarm and I was the only person in the office. I had to take care of communicating that it was not a real emergency and act as the point of contact. The branch manager at the time, a Mr. Powers, got into a bit of trouble since I was their representative. I was a vendor manager and not their management. It seems like I was the only person in a 100 person branch that put in the extra hours, day after day, week after week.

The Takeaway

Finally, remember every role in the organization is a *temporary* one. Your boss, her boss, and her boss's boss, they are all up for debate every financial quarter of every financial year, if not sooner. The worst mistake a team player can make is thinking she'll always be "just" a team player. The more you know every person's role on the team, and perform yours well, the more chances you'll have to be MVP of your *own* personal success story. Next I will tell about something you can start doing today that will help you. Ironically, it's a sport but it's not a team sport.

PLAY LIKE THE BOYS—
LEARN TO GOLF

"To find a man's true character, play golf with him."
—P.G. Wodehouse

L adies, if you want to advance your professional career you need to seriously consider learning to play golf. I can hear you chuckling at this all the way from my office. Yes, I did say golf. Daddy was right. I am sorry to be the one to tell you that golf is still a powerful business tool and lesson in reality. If your goal is to smash the glass ceiling you better learn how to swing a golf club. This is a sport that is tightly associated with business. Many high-ranking executives use golf for networking and for making deals, or, at a minimum, discussing details of the deal. In spite of knowing this, many women still don't consider golf crucial in business and this is a huge mistake.

So why aren't women giving golf its due? It could be that women still believe that advancement up the corporate ladder depends solely on their skills and experiences. This just isn't reality. Golf would be an excellent required course requirement for every MBA candidate. I don't know why it isn't. Many corporations actually suggest that their junior managers learn golf. Why wouldn't they when we know what we know about golf and business by simple observation? What do all the US Presidents do on vacation? They play golf. Point taken. If it's good enough for the Commander in Chief then it's good enough for you as an aspiring CEO. Take the cue.

How to Get in the Game

So what exactly is it that golf can do for you? Playing golf gives you the opportunity to prove yourself to your male colleagues and in some industries it can also improve your standing among clients. Golf irrefutably offers a way that women can spend more time and gain more access with *key, male decision makers*. We've already established that men are still running the business world, haven't we? We don't need to beat them, we have to join them. Furthermore as golf provides a handicap based on ability, everyone plays from a leveled playing field, regardless of ability, at least in theory. In other words it isn't a game where men are simply going to outmuscle you. Finesse and skill stands a chance.

Golf offers women the chance to earn the respect of men in a friendly way, to develop your network and connect to others in a less-threatening, more personal manner. Less threatening by far than, say, going out to a night club together, which is still a safe networking option for men in business. Many executive and aspiring executive women are still convinced that you can get ahead by hard work alone, but hard work will only get you so far. Today you need to be aware that for business it is just as important to be with the right people at the right place and in the right time. Often that time happens on the greens.

Some of the most powerful women in the world play golf both recreationally and for business. Former Secretary of State Condoleezza Rice, retired Supreme Court Justice Sandra Day O'Connor and Melinda Gates (of the Gates Foundation) all play golf. Patricia Woertz, Chairman and CEO of the Archer Daniels Midland Company and IBM CEO Virginia Rometty all play golf. Virginia Rometty was the third woman to join the Augusta National Golf Club, home to the Masters Golf Tournament.

The Augusta National Golf Club is one of the most famous golf clubs in the world. It was opened in January of 1933 with a strict no-women policy. This policy changed in August

2012 when the club admitted Condoleezza Rice and Darla Moore as its first two female members. This was a great day for women in sports but also for women in business. It makes you wonder if Conde Rice and George Bush sealed the deal for her appointment on a golf course somewhere. Doesn't it?

So how do you get started if you know nothing about golf? Here's how to start. If you already belong to a golf club, great! You've already got an in. Find the golf pro and take lessons and then invite your male colleagues and clients to your club.

If you don't belong to a club there are always public courses or you might look into joining a chapter of the Executive Women's Golf Association (EWGA) an association whose mission is to provide women with the opportunity to learn and play golf. The majority of EWGA's 20,000 members are between 36 and 55 years old, which makes them a prime target for networking. They'll help you find a golf instructor and people to play with. That's sure to give your career a boost even if you never develop a scratch game.

Field Notes

I'm not a great golfer, but I like to think I'm a fair golfer when I practice. To the detriment of my golfing time, lately I've been concentrating on tennis. To participate, I think women (or men for that matter) should just be at considered a fair player at their chosen sport. It is potentially important to their career, or to the business organization they are a part of. This might require taking some lessons.

Here's what being a "fair" player means to me:

- You are not a complete imbecile at the sport that causes embarrassment of your fellow team members;
- You don't delay the game with your lack of skill or knowledge;
- You can laugh at yourself and your short comings;
- You know and can appreciate the protocol or etiquette of the sport.

So I'll maintain I am a fair golfer. Anyone that plays golf with me will have a good time and enjoy the camaraderie, and in the end would likely welcome another golf date with me. That is enough to satisfy me.

On another note, in addition to golf, it's a good idea to learn about football. I love football. I know the game. I like watching it in the stadium or on TV and I love tail-gaiting. I can tell you the quarterbacks, running backs and coaches for the top teams and I genuinely enjoy discussing team stats with men in business or social settings. My father is a football fan so the game was on in our home quite often.

When conducting business it's important to find common ground. Whenever there is a lull in conversation, I can always talk about football. Although it's certainly not 100% of men in business who are NFL or AFL fans, I would estimate a good 80% of them are.

One thing I noticed early on in my career was that not many other businesswomen appreciated the NFL so this made me of a novelty in the mostly, male-dominated conversations. Today football is a pastime enjoyed more evenly by both sexes and in fact during football season, I can count on most of my Monday conference calls leading in with talk about last night's game. Still, if you want a leg up-engaging with men, you might want to know a bit about the NFL.

The Takeaway

If you just cannot manage golf or talking about football, you can still look for other ways to participate in sports. There is no reason why you can't form similar connections with people at the baseball field, on the tennis court, or even out for a jog. US Masters Swimming has over 50,000 members who participate in swim practices weekly and by running meets and other competitive and social activities. Many people enjoy joining clubs to train for bike races and triathlons. These activities are tremendously popular among top-ranking business people who enjoy testing their mettle competitively outside the office. Find a sport that works for you because sport provides a terrific elixir for networking and talking business, particularly with men.

THE IMPORTANCE OF MENTOR RELATIONSHIPS

"In learning you will teach and in teaching you will learn."

—Singer Phil Collins

"Leaders…should influence others…in such a way that it builds people up, encourages and edifies them so they can duplicate this attitude in others."

—Bob Goshen

In addition to inviting change and using the tools and concepts I've provided in this book, the other crucial message I'd like you to takeaway is that finding a mentor is one of the most important things you'll ever do as an aspiring female executive. Then, once you have made it to management, giving back by mentoring another young woman who's just entered the workforce will be one of the most rewarding and important roles you will fulfill in your leadership.

This relationship is so valuable because a mentor can provide you with feedback, insight and inspiration. She can act as your devil's advocate, a helping hand, a sounding board, wisdom whisperer and so much more. A mentor will push you beyond your comfort zone so that you can grow. Yet, in spite of all these benefits, we women still struggle to find mentors and get things started.

As women, many of us find it hard to ask for help. We know that mentoring takes valuable time, effort, energy and resources. We wonder how we can ever repay a mentor who invests so much in us. How do we ask someone to commit to something out of pure altruism? Why would someone even want to help us? This chapter will help illuminate not only the role of mentors, but how, where and even why to find them. Relax. Most people who offer to mentor have had a few good mentors themselves and they understand the value of this relationship. Once someone has "made it," they want to give back and they are usually more than happy to mentor others.

Business Mentors Who Have Helped Me

I've mentioned my good fortune in having had such wonderful childhood mentors. I've also been fortunate to have had them in my career. I met my first business mentor immediately after I started my software company. Her name was Robyn Button, of Portland Oregon. What was wonderful about Robyn was that she was a seemingly "emotionless" manager. She was highly organized, highly articulate and without a doubt she commanded respect in a softened way with clients. You might know women like this. They are the ones who seem to be a step above the rest in their communications with the client. These were the women I deliberately chose as mentors and sought to emulate.

Here some of what I learned directly from Robyn (her wisdom addresses many of the topics discussed in this book):

- There are ways to frame a question, ways to move a project forward, ways to treat people both those above and below the job title with respect and kindness.
- Being stern or talking louder than your male counterparts isn't a show of strength but an indication of weakness.

- Women have to learn to work smart while sometimes it seems men just need to have a good network.
- The bathroom is for crying not the conference room whenever you're upset over an unfair policy or bad decisions or just in frustration.
- "ANGER is just one letter away from DANGER"… from Sesame Street back in the 1970s when Colorado College started broadcasting it
- Anytime you lose your sense of calm and become angry everyone will stop listening to you and you will lose credibility.

Robyn took me under her wing. She recognized my youth and enthusiasm for management and she guided me expertly through the swirling waters of the Macy's corporate environment. It was Robyn who helped me to navigate through the layers of internal management. As Robyn did for me, a great mentor can help you achieve greater success and growth in so many ways. A mentor will help you develop more confidence and she will help you learn the skills to help you become the businesswoman you've always wanted to be. This is exactly what Robyn did for me, she taught me many lessons I did not have to learn through mistakes. I will always be grateful to her.

What defines a Great Mentor? Why do you need one?

One of the biggest tragedies in business, and in life, is that many people (women in particular) often stop their pursuit of formal learning once they leave school. Of course, in the technology sector this can never happen. Whether it's after finishing high school, college, graduate school or after getting an MBA, many of us mistakenly get to a point where we think we are equipped enough to just let life take over and learn passively.

I'm not sure exactly why this is. It may simply be that we become overburdened juggling work and home life. Whatever the cause, what a bad idea this is! There is still so much more to learn! Finding a mentor can not only help you continue your education but it will propel you forward in ways you never imagined possible. Here is another area where you can invite change by allowing a mentor to help you. Working with a mentor shifts your professional learning from passive attendance to proactive, active engagement.

When you are looking to enter a mentor relationship—just as when you consider entering any other kind of relationship—you want to be cautious and evaluating. Not every potential mentor will work out for you. Finding and cultivating a truly great mentor relationship will take time and effort.

Here are a number of qualities to look for in a mentor:

- **Specific Area of Expertise.** You want a mentor who is an expert in their field.
- **Great Communicator.** You want a mentor who is an effective communicator so you can easily absorb their knowledge.
- **Willing.** Seek a mentor who demonstrates a truly passionate willingness to share what they know with you.
- **Patient.** Any mentor must be able to be patient with you as you go about the learning process.
- **Available.** Even the best mentor is worthless if you never have access to them! Make sure to look for a mentor who has the time and availability that you need to meet regularly.
- **Compatible.** Be sure to find a mentor you are compatible with, otherwise you'll find yourself at odds and waste both of your time. Like any relationship, if it's too much of a struggle move on.
- **Inspirational.** Mentors ought to inspire you to see beyond the limitations you may hold for yourself or, just as commonly, any rut(s) you may have gotten yourself into.
- **Educational.** Mentors can help you continue your education long after school, by encouraging you to

learn new skill sets and offering practical advice on how to obtain them.

- **Motivational**. Mentors motivate you to stay on track, particularly when you have regular meetings, updates, spot checks and consultations with them.
- **Experienced**. Mentors offer their own personal, unique and individual experience to help you avoid some of the mistakes they've made as you follow your own path to success.

Mentors can advise you in untold ways in order to help you achieve your goals. So as you begin to search for your own mentor—or mentors—be sure to keep these qualities in mind. And now that you know what to look for *in* a mentor, let's help you find one!

Where to Look for a Mentor

"Mentoring is a brain to pick, an ear to listen, and a push in the right direction."
—John C. Crosby

We've already discussed the scarcity of women in the ranks of leadership. This doesn't mean you can't find a good female mentor. You just need to know where to look and, of course, where not to look. We are all perpetually busy, and since most mentors work on a "volunteer" basis, getting someone to commit to regular meetings can be challenging at best even once you do find one. Don't let this discourage you. Anyone who is willing to mentor you delights in sharing their passion for their work with you.

Here are some ideas on where to find a mentor:

- **Look around your workplace.** Start where you are by looking inside your workplace for someone wise and willing. Find a woman in a leadership position such as a manager or coworker who has been there a while. Do you have a colleague you'd like to learn more about? Is there someone in your office in a role that you aspire to? What if you were to invite that someone to lunch or coffee?

- **Branch Out.** If there is no one inside your company, how about a client's company or a similar company? Is there someone you know in passing, the owner of a similar business you frequent or local thought leader, who might be interested in mentoring you? Is there a shop or a business that where you really enjoy the management style and attention to customer service? Quite often if I find someone giving exceptional customer service I get their contact information or give them my card thinking I might offer them a job as a trainer. I hired one of our trainers like that.

- **Join women's business networking groups.** A great way to find wise, and willing, mentors is to join a networking group for women. Here you'll connect with a variety of women from varying industries and expertise levels, all with different skill sets you can pick up for yourself. Successful women typically like to mentor.

- **Go to seminars and listen to guest speakers.** Be active in your community and attend all the brown bag lunches, seminars, workshops and other educational opportunities you can. Here you'll find guest speakers with wit and wisdom to spare, many of whom might be willing to mentor you. You would be surprised as to how flattered and willing successful female speakers may be if you but ask them for their help to succeed in your career.

- **Search Churches or Religious Organizations.** There are a lot of women in clergy and leadership positions these days. Don't overlook them as possible mentors. They also usually know their congregation pretty well and they may be able to put you in touch with other potential mentors within the community.

- **Volunteer.** Volunteering either directly for a charity or indirectly through a woman's service organization like the Junior League will not only give you a great opportunity to work for a worthy cause but it will put you to shoulder to shoulder with other career women. The Junior League has a built-in mentor pool called their "Sustainers." Sustainers are women who are no longer required to participate in the regular activities and causes of the Junior League but who remain connected primarily as a resource to the younger members.
- **Ask for referrals.** It's ok to let friends and family know when you are looking for a mentor. Ask them who they know who might be an expert in the area you want to learn about. People who know you well might come up with great suggestions. Don't be afraid to ask.

As you can see, there are a variety of places to begin looking for mentors, but this list is by no means all-inclusive. The mentorship process is as individual as its participants, so if you think you know of a great place to find a mentor or a great mentor you'd like to pursue, go for it!

How to Nurture a Mentor Relationship

One sure way to sabotage a mentor-mentee relationship is by assuming that it's all take and no give. Like any working relationship, being a mentor and being mentored is a two-way street. It's giving and receiving, so that the relationship is a mutually beneficial one.

Here are a few simple tricks on how to work with a mentor:

- **Be flexible.** Consider your mentor's schedule when planning when, where and how often you meet.
- **Participate.** Being mentored is not the same as being lectured. It is up to you to run each meeting, either with questions, topics or an agenda to be explored. A mentor's time is valuable, so use it wisely!
- **Be prepared.** During each meeting, whether it's on the phone, via Skype/Webex or in person, always treat it like a business meeting. Be professional, be on time, be engaged, be invested and, above all, be prepared to make the most of your mentor's time. Preparation means that you know in advance what your "take away" will be.
- **Be a "Lady Who Lunches".** One way to return a mentor's wit and wisdom is with a little grub! If possible be sure to compensate a mentor with at least a free meal, cup of coffee or some other "treat" to make

your meetings a little more social. As women we usually know how to make meal times special, so be generous in your time and attention and compensation to your mentor. Small gifts of appreciation are also perfectly acceptable. It is not necessary, but some do pay for mentoring.

It's a bit of a controversy as to whether one should pay for a mentor. The relationship is typically a voluntary one. It's not that paying for a mentor wouldn't be valuable but it may change the feel of the exchange to more of a counseling or coaching relationship. The premise of a mentoring relationship relies upon the notion that an older, more experienced and accomplished person takes a vested interest in the livelihood and progress of someone more junior. Typically the junior is also, concurrently, likely to be less financially secure. It's not wrong to seek and pay for a mentor, but it's less common and certainly not necessary.

So, pay a mentor if you feel inclined, but rest assured you aren't required to. Remember that being mentored is a privilege, not a right. The more we can do to honor that relationship by giving of ourselves as much as we get back from our mentor, the better both participants will be in the long run. Expressing gratitude will surely encourage your mentor to want to continue helping you. Your success is likely to be enough in return.

Currently I am a certified mentor participating in the "Mentoring Women's Network," a national volunteer organization based in Indianapolis, Indiana. In addition, I mentor all the new team members within my company. Nothing makes me happier than to see another young woman taking her rightful place in the business world and succeeding.

Until You Find a Mentor, Seek Out Good Role Models

While seeking a mentor, keep an eye out for role models who may never become your mentor but have all the qualifications. This is what I call mastering "The Fine Art of Emulation." In other words, find a woman in your organization—a manager, team leader, colleague or even your CEO—and emulate her. This may seem unorthodox, but think about it, isn't imitation the sincerest form of flattery? Don't we tend to imitate those we find ideal, either personally or professionally? Imitation and assimilation leads to progress.

I think young women don't realize how often they emulate other women; dressing like each other, buying the same handbags as each other. There is also the sub-conscious or conscious emulation of our mothers, good or bad as that it might be.

I am very fortunate to have had a mother, Dianne C. Garcia, who possesses a number of qualities that I could emulated from very early on in my career. She is driven.

She has a determination to succeed. She is a multi-talented artist and an amazing gourmet chef. My mother is really an amazing women, she becomes an expert at anything she tries. She also rose above being looked down upon by her chauvinistic father because she was female. She ignored his low expectations for her and graduated from college. I know I got my liveliness and drive from her. For all this and more I remain be eternally grateful.

Emulation can take many forms:

- Listen carefully and try to learn verbal cues from those women you see as "ideals" of power, privilege or authority. Study them.
- Emulate what the powerful and intelligent women in your workplace read, which newsletters they follow and seminars they attend.
- Observe and adopt how they communicate with others.
- You can emulate how they dress, carry and comport themselves on a day-to-day basis.
- Adopt their sense of professionalism in their ability to separate business from personal.

Regardless of who you choose to emulate , and how, consider this as a way to be mentored... without the mentor! You can find many women to emulate, choosing the best aspects of female leaders to incorporate in your own professional brand or persona.

Field Notes:

I actively mentor all the employees I hire who ended up staying in my company for more than a couple of years. Currently I have an engineer that I've been "mentoring for about 11 years and she is thriving in her career. I've mentored younger cousins of mine and even felt I've mentored my younger sister in her career and management choices. I know that they have chosen to emulate me and I have a sense of honor about that.

I am also a volunteer through a mentoring program. Most recently I've been mentoring a young women who was seeking an audience with her VP. She needed help preparing for meetings with her direct manager and her director prior to that. Over a series of phone calls and "Starbuck's meetings" I provided her with how I thought the VP would view their conversation. I emphasized that her stated goals should be the same as the business goals not just an expression of her own needs. I suggested she end the meeting with an actionable item that her VP could easily agree to. Together we developed a plan of action and she executed it fully. We have a fondness for each other we have forged a friendship that I imagine will continue for many years.

The Takeaway

Being mentored is a wonderful way to embrace the spirit of intergenerational sharing, learning from others who have been where you want to go! You don't need do it on your own! Enlist the help of others, either through mentorship or emulation, and learn from the best to make your journey a little less rocky and your future a lot brighter! As we age, we start to think about what we leave behind. There are women who went before you who are ready and willing to pass you the baton. Take your time to find them.

PRACTICAL APPEARANCE MATTERS
A.K.A. DRESS FOR SUCCESS

"Dress shabbily, they notice the dress, dress impeccably they notice the woman."

—Coco Chanel

"I don't dress to fit in, I dress to stand out."

—Dr. Genevieve Bell

"Dress always, one notch above our client"

—ECS Employee Handbook

The first visible impression you make on clients, managers and co-workers is as important as what you have to say. What you wear and even your hairstyle can direct the impression of who you want to be in the corporate world. The simplest advice I can give you here is that just as you emulate the behavior and practices of the woman executive you want to be, you should learn to dress like her too.

When I went through training with IBM, I was taught early to "dress up" for clients. We were always expected to look the part of "Big Blue," in a sharp suit and heels, no matter how casual the client's culture was. This meant dressing impeccably. As business casual has become more popular I've learned that I can relax that a bit sometimes, but only in context. For example when we landed a NIKE contract, we took cues from their environment and discovered that khakis and more casual shoes were just fine with them.

Today, telecommuters work in their pajamas and we never know what to expect in the background during a videoconference. The business environment has changed—a lot. However, regardless of the organization or the year, there are still some perpetual standards that never change about the way women should dress in the workplace. It would seem that everyone would know how to dress, but sadly, it isn't.

Here are a few tips for when you're flying into a business meeting or flying your way straight to the top:

- **Over or Under?** It's always better to be overdressed than underdressed. If the environment is casual and you are in a crisp suit, you will carry authority. If the environment is very formal and you are casual, you'll immediately lose credibility.
- **Dress appropriately for the occasion.** By all means if a client invites you to the company picnic, you can dress down a bit. But it's still no license to let it all hang out. If you are normally impeccable but show up in a pair of cutoffs to a corporate event that would be very bad and few would forget it.
- **Designer doesn't always make it appropriate**. Don't be fooled into thinking that because something is designer it's ok for the office. Nowadays, the word "Juicy" appears on just about everything. You do not want to be "Juicy" or "Pink" in a business setting. Enough said here. The flip side of this is that you don't have to buy designer to look good either. You just need to be polished. If you are low on funds, you can learn to shop bargains and sales.
- **Clothing talks.** What does your wardrobe say? Always make sure you are sending the right message. If you work with other women, it's easy to discern protocol if you look to your superiors and co-workers. Dress like your superiors! Caution: If you work in a male-

dominated environment, don't look to the guys for guidance on whether something is appropriate. Men may not be honest with you. They might tell you that you can be taken seriously in tight or very short garments. But they won't take you seriously and it will cause a big distraction. That's not the sort of attention you want if you are looking to move up to management.

- **How low can you go?** There's always a question regarding décolleté. Women who are busty need to take care to beware of showing too much. Again, and especially considering the proximity of your bust to your face, you needn't cover up entirely, but be tasteful. Make sure that you can maintain eye contact with the men you are doing business with. That is if you want their contract, not their personal cellular number.

- **How high, how much thigh?** If you've got nice legs, there's no harm in showing off a little. Your legs spend a lot of time parked under the desk so why not make the most of those walks down the hall? This is one area you can be a little freer as the fashion of skirt lengths does go up and down. However, be careful never to go too tight or too short. Definitely make sure that everything that needs to stay out of sight does.

- **Use color.** You will still see a lot of the blue, the black and the grey in corporate, legal, accounting and engineering offices. Thankfully, women can get away with more colorful clothing. But don't go too loud with your colors or too crazy with your prints! To add a splash of color and interest do it with a scarf or with a bright blouse under a jacket. Men make statements with neckties that add a pop of color and you can too. Here is advice on using a scarf to make a statement. "One piece of clothing equals one word in a sentence," says Mirella Zanatta, associate director of programs at brand consulting company Corporate Class Inc. in Toronto, Ontario. Wearing the right scarf in the right way will make you appear to be a refined person who has put thought into your outfit," said Zanatta, who is also president of the Canadian chapter of the Association of Image Consultants International. ("Morrison, Lennox. "Is this the New Power Symbol for Women? BBC Capital. March 20, 2015. Accessed April 1, 2015. (http://www.bbc.com/capital/story/20150319-the-power-symbol-for-women.)

- **Hair, tattoos, piercings, body jewelry.** The late 1990's and the 2000's have brought great popularity to the fashion of getting your body inked and pierced. Unfortunately what you thought was a great idea when you were 18 isn't always a great idea when you are 24 and trying to land a serious job. If you have a tattoo that is nicely out of sight, it's none of my business. Let's keep it that way!

Field Notes

I did hire a young woman with a tattoo on her leg and I asked her to always make sure she always wore a suit with pants. I remember working on a contract with the FBI in San Diego. The weather was warm and she was the only one of us in pants. This may seem harsh but she was happy to comply. Our clients are international as well and we need to keep it in mind that what's culturally innocuous here may be quite another thing in another country. For example, in Japan, a woman with a tattoo is considered a "lady of the evening." One executive I know who has a tattoo is always sure to cover it when she travels to Japan.

I also nearly hired a gal with a very small nose stud (a diamond) and told her she would have to remove it if she worked for us. We didn't hire her so it didn't come up. I tell my new hires that our clients spend upwards of 6-digits for their new telecommunications systems, and they expect that we will represent their company in a manner that reflects their corporate culture. This means if my company represents IBM, we should dress and look the way IBM's own employees do.

The Takeaway

None of the new employees I've hired have ever had trouble complying with my dress code. In fairness, I balance my demands. When I started my company in the late 1990's, I provided all my new hires with a cash advance for their clothing. I would tell them to go to "Ann Taylor" or "Casual Corner" and just buy suits. Then I would take it out of their first few pay checks at about $500 each pay check for a couple of months until it was paid off. It was a great way to show my new hires I was completely invested in their success and also a great way to place some control on how they dressed.

NEVER DRINK COFFEE
BEFORE A BUSINESS MEETING

"Never drink too much coffee while in any type of meeting because once you excuse yourself to the bathroom the males in the room will talk about you and form a bond that will exclude you in decisions."

—Robyn Button

S o here is just why I say "Never drink coffee before a business meeting." No doubt you've been wondering about it since you picked up this book. To answer, it began as just this one piece of advice that I got from one of my mentors, Robyn Button. It's exactly the sort of thing that I might have discovered on my own but was fortunate I didn't have to. But is it really just this simple when it comes to coffee? As it turns out, there are other, more scientific reasons why you may want to re-think that third cup as you head into a meeting.

First, I confess, I'm a full-fledged Starbucks aficionado. I even tell my clients how Starbucks is basically my religion. I became a Starbucks "gold" member as soon as I realized that every nine punches on their "app" would earn me the 10th latte free. I typically don't get coffee anywhere else if I can help it. Adding to my loyalty to them is that Starbucks was once a client. For years I also bought my groceries at Fred Meyer/Kroger and my sports gear at NIKE because these too were clients of the first telecommunications company I founded. Just as I try to stay loyal and shop in my local community I'm loyal to my clients and patronize them whenever possible.

Our engagement with Starbucks headquarters is a fun one to look back on it. They had a company policy that all their vendors had to have some of their staff trained to use the free barista stations located on each floor of their headquarters. My design engineers at the time, saw this as an awesome perk while I ended up paying for them to be trained to make lattes for me and the rest of our team! I remember a sense of happiness within my team while we were onsite at Starbucks and for some odd reason our productivity went through the roof.

In all seriousness we appreciated the decorum of the Starbucks management and non-management and I also recall one of the Starbucks analysts was so impressed with one of our team member's performance that she later tried to "hire" her away from our firm (this never happened).

So that's just a little aside. Regarding coffee, when I relocated to Tampa, Florida, I switched my habit from one hot latte in the morning in Seattle to one hot "triple-venti-3-Splenda latte" in the morning and a "trenta, green-tea, cool-lime refresher" every afternoon, a horribly expensive addiction!

I've become acutely aware of the effect caffeine has on me. I'm already a fast-thinking, fast-talking take-charge kind of woman. I always need to remember to schedule an outlet for the extreme amounts of caffeine I can sometimes take in. Putting in extra-long hours to accomplish three days' worth of work in one day, or heading to an extra-long workout helps me burn off all the caffeinating. However when I'm meeting a new client, when I need to sit in on a key conference or when I am taking care to make a great first-impression, I'll limit myself to regular coffee and I deny myself that extra "triple shot" of caffeine.

Early in my career I had to learn to practice "slowing down" my speech so my clients or management partners could stay with me and follow my ideas. This came after a few failed attempts to be persuasive on some important projects. I learned that perhaps I wasn't making sense because my rapid fire communication style was too challenging for others to follow. In recognizing this about myself I learned I need to be careful about coffee intake. The last thing my communication speed needs is excessive caffeine. How about you? Have you examined how your thought process and communications operate with or without caffeine?

So I am still loving my coffee but I've delving deeper into its affects. Dr. Travis Bradberry, M.D. who has published studies on coffee, business performance and Emotional Intelligence showing there's evidence of a dark side to coffee, especially when it comes to business performance. The results from his studies have appeared in Forbes, The Huffington Post and many other business publications and they are worth considering.

Bradberry contends "The ability to manage your emotions and remain calm under pressure has a direct link to your performance...90 percent of top performers are high in emotional intelligence. These individuals are skilled at managing their emotions (even in times of high stress) in order to remain calm and in control." And Bradberry's studies show that coffee isn't helping with this.

Bradberry continues, "Drinking caffeine triggers the release of adrenaline. Adrenaline is the source of the "fight or flight" response, a survival mechanism that forces you to stand up and fight or run for the hills when faced with a threat. The fight-or-flight mechanism sidesteps rational thinking in favor of a faster response. This is great when a bear is chasing you, but not so great when you're responding to a curt email. When caffeine puts your brain and body into this hyper-aroused state, your emotions overrun your behavior." (Bradberry, Travis, MD. "Caffeine: The Silent Killer of Success." The Huffington Post. January 26, 2015. Accessed May 10, 2015. http://www.huffingtonpost.com/dr-travis-bradberry/caffeine-the-silent-kille_b_6179708.html).

We've talked a lot about the importance of controlling your emotions in business haven't we? Here Bradberry cautions that coffee may be working against your maintaining emotional control and subsequently sabotaging your success!

Bradberry also says that the reason we feel sharp and bright after a cup of coffee isn't really due to the caffeine but to the refueling of our caffeine addiction! Bradberry continues, "New research from Johns Hopkins Medical School shows that performance increases due to caffeine intake are the result of caffeine drinkers experiencing a short-term reversal of caffeine withdrawal…Caffeine-related performance improvement is nonexistent without caffeine withdrawal. In essence, coming off caffeine *reduces* your cognitive performance and has a negative impact on your mood. The only way to get back to *normal* is to drink caffeine, and when you do drink it, you feel like it's taking you to new heights. In reality, the caffeine is just taking your performance back to normal for a short period."

Wow! I know about this feeling. If you drink coffee you probably do too. Caffeine, I believe, puts me in a good mood. It makes me feel like I can do anything. It makes me happy about life in general. But here, real science is saying that isn't exactly how it works. It's definitely something to consider.

So I am not saying don't drink coffee ever. In truth as I hit the 40's, I've found my mornings just don't start until I've had my first cup. While training for my first full marathon, I even perfected my own method of running with my Starbucks latte, to the amazement of my friends. What I'm saying is that if you drink coffee directly before or during your business meetings there might be consequences you didn't anticipate or bargain for.

On the serious side you may be continuing on a vicious cycle of caffeine addiction and relief and on the practical side, as my mentor pointed out to me so long ago, it might require your having to excuse yourself mid-conference. What you might miss could affect you greatly. Decisions made in your absence might determine your influence or lack thereof or could lead your project in an entirely difference direction.

In the worst case scenario you could be left out of a decision that would have been key to your advancement. We have all been in meetings when one variable changes in the meeting and the entire conference takes a new tone. You don't want to be absent from the room at that key moment. And, in a caffeinated hyper-arousal state and you risk losing your cool. These are some very good reasons to be careful with coffee.

Field Notes:

Here is a good example of what happened in a recent meeting I was attending. A particular project we had been on, had some rather inexperienced project managers running it. We were discussing whether our team should take on the client's new requirement for "advance" end user training. The primary project manager issued a directive saying that "perhaps" the team should not take this engagement on. Within milliseconds consensus followed from the other junior project managers it seemed decision had been made. In these five seconds if I had visited the ladies room due to excessive coffee drinking it would be have been settled but since I was there I could turn it around. I was familiar with this team of managers so even after this "consensus" was made, I calmly brought up the idea that perhaps at this stage with the client our team should leave every opportunity open. Instead of passing, we gained this engagement and it's been profitable.

The Takeaway

This is the way it works in group dynamics. Sometimes when a decision is offered and if even one person backs it, it sticks whether or not it is the right and sound thing to do for the team. For this reason you should never leave a meeting for any reason. Decisions made without you can affect your career, your team or your company. So there you have it. Never drink coffee before or during a business meeting! However, of course you can drink it after.

WHEN TO GO FOR IT: BECOMING COMFORTABLE TAKING RISKS

"Women need to shift from thinking 'I'm not ready to do that' to thinking 'I want to do that and I'll learn by doing it.'"

—Sheryl Sandberg

"It's impossible to live without failing unless you live so cautiously that you might not have lived at all, in which you fail by default."

—J.K. Rowling

R isk is a part of life. Working at an office, working at home, your commute; it all entails a certain amount of risk. In the past two decades, the stock market crashed and then the real estate bubble burst. Entire industries were wiped out. Along with these events went any hope the rest of us had for career stability. Today, risk seems more a part of life than ever. For certain women, however, risk is not something they associate with fear. Instead, it is something they equate with opportunity. If that's you and Katy Perry's "Roar" is your anthem already great! If you're not there yet, you can learn to embrace risk.

Julie Zeilinger writes in "7 Reasons Why Risk-Taking Leads To Success," for the Huffington Post saying, "We tend to view risk-taking negatively, often regarding it as dangerous and even unwise. But while some risks certainly don't pay off, it's important to remember that some do." Zeilinger suggests, "Reframing risk as an opportunity to succeed rather than a path to failure."

In her article, Zeilinger discusses Sandra Peterson, CEO of the $10 billion business "Bayer Crop Science," adding, "Most women I know who have been successful in business; it's because they've been willing to take on the risky challenge that other people would say, 'Oh, I'm not sure I want to do that." I can certainly relate to that. I can't tell you the number of times friends of mine have told me that I was "brave" or I was "courageous" simply because I was willing to take a risk in some way that they deemed impossible.

When we talk about "going for it," what we're usually talking about is considering an endeavor that involves a certain amount of risk and doing it anyway. For instance, each time we ask for a promotion, we risk upsetting the apple cart of the status quo relationship we have with our boss or the status quo of our "position" in the organization. Same with asking for a raise, time off, maternity leave or whatever it may be. These aren't big risks, but for many women they're enough to keep them from "going for it," often indefinitely.

Other, bigger risks might include: applying for a whole new position, moving to a whole new department, going to night school to learn a new profession or even leaving our present company to work for one where more opportunities exist for women in general. Even if the position may offer less compensation. Regardless of the size, nature or complexity of the risk, one thing is certain: there is a right time and place to "go for it".

Apply for Opportunity Whenever it Presents Itself—Repeat
One of the biggest misconceptions we have about business is that we only get one shot to make our mark. After all, we've all heard the phrase "opportunity only knocks once," but the explosion of entrepreneurs in recent years has laid waste to that

particular truism. In fact, according to one of the globe's ultimate entrepreneurs, Richard Branson, "Business opportunities are like buses, there's always another one coming." Let's toss out the idea of only one knock and replace it with the notion that like fish in the ocean idea, opportunities are as vast and far reaching as the number of fish in the sea. Your job is to seek them out. It's time to get fishing!

Do good opportunities exist within your current organization? Or do you feel like your ship has already sailed and you're stuck in a dead end job because you weren't paying attention when opportunity knocked the first time?

In order to put your more opportunities on your career radar, more often, follow these simple steps:

- **Pay attention.** Some of the best opportunities that exist for women in the modern workplace are the simple learning opportunities that take place every day. A new skill, a new habit, a new statistic or detail, these can all merge to create opportunity for you—either today or tomorrow.
- **Make it a habit**. Work every day to see the opportunity that exists all around you. Don't just trash the company newsletter, read it instead! Don't just delete every internal email you get, take the time to read them and decipher if an opportunity exists amidst the clutter and

junk. It's easy to get sidetracked by looking over your current cubicle to that "next big thing," but where you are could be the "current big thing," if only you'd focus on your own performance and not what the other guy or gal is doing to get ahead.

- **Get in the habit of asking**. Many people, women in particular, are afraid to ask for anything. We want to be seen as so self-sufficient you could drop us on a deserted island and we'd still have those slides collated, color treated, proofed and formatted by the three o'clock meeting! But asking is a sure way to show interest, learn things, network, reach out, grow and expand your reach.

It may not seem like opportunity comes around every day, but if you pay attention, look closely and open yourself up to the possibility of all potential moves, we'll see that there is always some way for you to influence and create our own new opportunities. You just need to be willing to look and, when needed, leap. In the words of John Burroughs "Leap and the net will appear."

Aspire to another Potential, Not another Position

It is important to be able to discern between *positions* and *potentials*. A simple position; secretary, assistant office manager, office manager, regional office manager, etc., may a temporary opportunity, one that generally exists to move us from Point A to Point B and later from Point B to Point C. Is this really the case?

When we have a "potential mindset," we don't just view the next rung on the corporate ladder as a position, but as the potential to learn, grown, achieve, network, learn and succeed. I know a woman who is a TV producer now who began the station working the switchboard. She didn't see her time as a receptionist as a dead-end but as a means to an end. Internships, paid or unpaid, also offer a glimpse as to whether an entry-level position can become a means to an end.

Some of us don't see the opportunities at our workplace because we've gotten ourselves into a holding pattern. We're biding time until someone promotes us. OK, maybe working as an assistant office manager isn't what we want to be doing forever—nor is assistant sales manager, cashier, clerk or marketing rep—but when we see every position as a potential to prove ourselves, we tend to outshine our competition and perform beyond expectations. When we do this, we can ask for the next position and create the next potential instead of *waiting* for someone to hand it to us. The point is to do your best at whatever your role is and keep reaching.

Emulate the Person in the Position You Want

One way to go beyond your current status in your department is to work "as if" you already have the position you want, not the position you have. In other words, if your role as assistant marketing representative consists of five duties, why stop there? Do all five of those duties—handling incoming calls, managing existing accounts, drafting ad copy, etc.—with flair and verve and you can go beyond. Learn what the actual marketing representative does. If you watch the managers who have the positions you want, you see clearly their responsibilities and their actions. When you imitate them in your own way, it proves to you and to the organization you have these same capabilities. Actions always speak louder. Charge ahead, accomplish more goals and up your game by actively deciding to not stay below the radar. What are the things you can do now to get yourself noticed?

Here are some simple ways to go beyond your current job description to turn the job you have into the job you want:

- **Take your time.** One reason you may initially get turned down for something is that you simply jumped the gun. It's easy to forget that, in addition to our own personal and professional needs, the company has needs of its own. The more you understand those needs and work toward them, the more you learn in every position you fulfill. Growth takes time, and so does success. We all want to be somewhere a little further along than we currently are, but oftentimes we're where we are for a reason. Often, that reason is to learn the skills we'll need to take that next step—when the time is right.

- **Learn the Corporate Culture.** Every office has politics, every team has a vibe and every team member is unique. Every organization has a pace, a rhythm, a flow and a way of doing things that is unique to the company. It may not be the way they did things in your old company, or even on your old team at the same company. So before going for it, take some time to learn the culture and understand how others have achieved success within that particular organizational structure, flow, pace and rhythm. This also means getting to know all the players and their positions in the company.

- **Know how you fit.** We all wear two hats at work—our individual hat, and our team player hat. As a team member we each have a particular fit within the department or organization. What's yours? When you know how you fit in you are more prepared to seize opportunities that develop for when they are *right* for *you*.

- **Work your magic.** Finally, get to know "you." In other words, know your strengths, know your weaknesses, know what makes you special, valuable and unique and use those specific qualities to excel in whatever position you currently have in order to seek the position you ultimately want.

- **Establish your "Brand".** It's all the rage these days. Know yourself, promote yourself, and your unique skills.

Naturally, every workplace is different and some managers sincerely want to keep you "in your place" so that you can fit within their current organizational structure and culture. However, I've never met a CEO who faulted an employee for working beyond her potential each and every time!

The Worst They Can Say is "No"

Finally, you need to get comfortable with taking risks. "No" is *not* the worst word in the human language. In fact, sometimes, it's the answer you need to hear at just the right time. There have been many times in my life where I wasn't, technically speaking, qualified to take the next step in my career. I needed something—people skills, technical skills, and an additional level of management training—to take me to that next level. But if I'd never ask, I would have never found out what exactly was needed to advance. So risk, ask and learn.

Here is an exercise to help you get comfortable dealing with "no". Let's say you go in to your manager with the following questions and you are ready with a prepared responses:

You: "Do you think I'm ready to take over as technical lead?"

Manager: "No."

Your Reply: "Well, what exactly are the reasons that you think I am not ready for this role? This is what I'd like to be doing and I'd love your input on what you think I need to focus on to get there?"

You: "Do you think I'm ready to take on more employee direct reports?"

Manager: "No."

Your Reply: "Ok, I just wanted to let you know that I do have some time and ability to take on more projects and I'd like to grow in responsibility."

You: "Do you think I'm ready to lead the next big project?

Manager: "No."

Your Reply: "I didn't think so but I want to tell you that one day that's my goal. I will be happy to listen to any advice you can share with me on how to get there."

Sometimes, it's not the question you're asking, but how you ask it that makes all the difference. Asking for a promotion two months after you've just started a new assignment is too a big risk for most people. However, asking for "more responsibility" is a question that often meets with a resounding, "Yes!" Remember, the worst they can say is "no," and sometimes hearing "no" today means hearing "yes" tomorrow.

Hearing "no" is truly not the worst thing that can happen to you. Moreover, "no" doesn't need to be a dead end or a conversation stopper if you are prepared to ask why you are getting a "no" and how you can turn it into a "yes". Meanwhile, you've let your superiors know that you are hungry to move up and you're motivated to be a top performer. Then, when you do acquire what's needed to move up, make sure to blow your own horn and let everyone know what you've accomplished.

Field Notes

Learn from your lessons and mine! There's a lot of talk about "lessons learned" and "best practices" in business. I remember once when I was a project manager for a job with a large university and these concepts were still pretty new. I had printed out multiple page of "Lessons Learned" and began to address the project team. As I led the review of each item (each was significant and enlisted team participation feedback and discussion) I remembered noticing a key stakeholder in the conference squirming. Later this person casually mentioned that our list seemed rather large and perhaps it reflected negatively on the project in some way. This was years ago and again it was when this concept was new to corporate America so I can understand there might have been some confusion on his part. But even then I remember thinking, "How can any form of improvement that focuses on what went wrong be a bad thing?"

Certainly we agree today that identifying and learning from mistakes is not only a good thing, it's strategic. In business today it is perfectly acceptable to make mid-stream corrections or abandon projects before or even near completion—all for the purpose of saving or making money. The most important thing about doing this, however, is to make sure that all the mistakes you made are never repeated. This requires you to examine all the elements that shaped the direction things took and to identify all the obstacles so that you'll never have a repeat. This is the basis of good project management. Corporations have learned a lot from the concept of "cutting your losses."

The Takeaway

It's easy for people to say they've learned from past mistakes but to truly change your behavior due to them is the key. When you look at some of the most successful executives or entrepreneurs what they have in common is a penchant for examining their mistakes, commonly referred to as "failures" by the public. They take what they learned the hard way to shape their next success.

Going for it can be scary. Risk means change, and change means learning, and learning means growth. Growth is good. If you keep your eyes on the prize and recognize that no job is without risk, change or obstacles, then it makes "going for it" all the easier—and your chances of actually getting what you want that much greater!

STAYING RELEVANT IN BUSINESS

"If we move through the world inviting change, inviting discovery we invite opportunity in its purest form knowing confidently that change will provide success...."
—Liza Marie Garcia

C hange is not only the norm today. It always has been. Technology just seems to be accelerating change exponentially. The benefit of change is that it offers the constant opportunity for growth and improvement. The drawback of change is that even though we all know that change is inevitable, all too often we fear it. A strategy that works in business is to not only strive to manage change but to invite it and some cases even cause it.

Here is an example of a company that purposely brought change to the betterment and comfort of their employees:

A handful of executives at Bruner-Cox, a regional accounting and business consulting firm based in Canton, Ohio, read about how the increased use of computers and other electronic devices in the workplace was causing repetitive stress injuries. It was a problem once thought to only affect factory workers and laborers. So their management decided to study the company's employees as they worked to see if they were at risk. "We had people sitting at keyboards during tax season for maybe 12 hours," said one manager." Those observations turned into the first phase of a company-funded research project that brought body-friendly changes to the Bruner-Cox offices.

One of the first things they did was provide employees with laptop computers—a staple in an accounting firm—with big-screen monitors, standard-size, ergonomically correct keyboards and special mice. They added adjustable keyboard trays that can be raised 10 inches above the work surface, allowing workers to stand and type.

The company did more. They installed lighting in the ceilings to reduce glare and task lighting at each work station. Up went panels made of a sound-absorbing material to control noise, another obstacle to productivity. The most noticeable improvement for some employees was the chairs. Bruner-Cox replaced its hodgepodge of seating with new state-of-the-art chairs with flipper arms that moved up and down and rotated 360 degrees and backs that adjusted independently of one another. "Every piece on this chair is completely adjustable," said one manager, "It looks like something out of Star Trek."(Thompson, Lynn. "Inviting Change." Smart Business. July, 22, 2002. Accessed February, 2015. http://www.sbnonline.com/article/inviting-change-a-local-accounting-firm-confronts-the-prospect-of-repetitive-stress-injuries-head-on/.)

This is what I mean when I talk about inviting change. The management of this company did not wait until they had injury complaints to answer. They didn't hide from a potential threat to company productivity. They took positive action to prevent it. It would have been acceptable to simply wait until they had a critical mass of uncomfortable or injured employees before investing in ergonomic improvements. After all, there's that old adage, "If it isn't broken, don't fix it." But they chose to invite and cause change.

Imagine you were one of those employees facing down tax season but you had a great new chair and desk configuration? Wouldn't you feel very grateful to management and respond with willingness to go the extra mile in return? My guess is the company recouped their investment here many times over. This is but one example of inviting change versus managing change.

We have seen through history constancy of change. If you are just starting your career you will learn that you may change companies, positions and maybe even the cities that you work in. Your ability to adapt to change will become a measure of your success. But what if you *seek* out the change for your career *instead* of just adapting to change as it comes your way. This is what we try to do as a company and this is what it means when we talk about "inviting change."

Here are some ideas for areas where you can solicit change:

- **Applications.** Is there a new software application, platform, operating system or other technology that would dramatically streamline your business processes?
- **Training.** Is there training available that would augment the talents of your workforce to potentially boost their productivity? Is there training in another area or technology platform.
- **Policies.** Are your company policies getting a little outdated? Why not be the first in your industry to offer telecommuting three days a week or to provide on-site day care? Change with the needs of your changing workforce.
- **Hardware and equipment.** Would your bottom line get a boost from updates and upgrades to your equipment?

- **Know what the competition is doing.** Investigate your competitor's services and see how you can improve upon them.
- **Seek innovation.** Put together mini "think tank" sessions to examine new solutions to existing company issues.

These are just a few to get you thinking. This is, of course, not all-inclusive. The main point is that change doesn't need to be a reactive response. It can be proactive. Instead of waiting to manage change, you can embrace change and guide it to your advantage.

Field Notes

A big change I encouraged within my company was to actively develop Subject Matter Experts (SME's) within our specific disciplines I did this well ahead of when people even had heard of this concept. The genesis of this was due to a project where all the demands fell to one software design engineer. It seemed like a logical idea to take some of the load off his plate and assign or delegate specific areas to another engineer. This was a change for the client who now had multiple points of contact, not just the primary engineer and this was a change for the project management team as well. However they adjusted and eventually changed their management requirements due to this change which also lead to the development of the SME's and it has worked out as intended.

Our observation is that our competitors still "burn out" their engineers on large or complex projects while we employ this delegated approach. Our SME's specialize in areas like call center or telco management, for example. I believe this is unique to our company, within our industry. It's an approach that relieves the burden on the primary engineer and takes advantage of the team driven concept of success.

The Takeaway

So I've presented a lot of ideas about how women can take advantage of "lessons learned" from other women in business. I've shared some of my own lessons learned through mentors and through the writings and studies of those who advocate the advancement of women the workplace.

We have identified the many challenges women face and how to work around them, to our individual and mutual satisfaction, so we can build and enjoy lasting, upward-moving careers. As women we continue to work hard to improve and create opportunities for continuous growth and ascension, for ourselves and for each other. Collectively, we still have some pretty big challenges and inequities to overcome, but overcome them we will. Our next step is always how to take it to the next level by asking, "What change can we invite?"

Corporations and organizations of all types (athletic programs, academic, cultural) are all hierarchies. In most organizations, it is easy to distinguish between the beginner levels and the highest levels. One characteristic typical of CEO's and top executives is that we pride ourselves in our ability to bring our entire organization to the next level. How about the next and the next and to a level that never existed before?

The next level for a small business CEO might be winning the first $10 million contract. For an executive, it could be a promotion from Director to Vice President. For an entrepreneur, the next level may require continually adapting and affecting change in their organization in order to increase profit margins and gain market share. For a more junior, lower-level person it may be a move to an entry-level management position.

So, what happens when you finally get to the top level? How do you hold your position? As the saying goes, there's only one way to go from the top and that's down! Who is it in your organization is defining the top and when you've reached it? Is it your CEO? The President? Your board of directors?

It is my belief that the top is always shifting. There is *always* a new level reach or create. The way that you get there and stay there is through constant goal setting and re-setting and re-examining. Many companies moved through a tremendous amount of change during the last recession. We've learned and observed that all things constantly change. Your business can't reach the top or hope to remain there until your company adopts the mindset and corporate culture which can not only be responsive to but can actively invite change to itself.

So, what do I mean when I say "invite" change? I mean to actively *search it out*. I mean to welcome all the things and anything that could impact any part of your business or your career each and every day, however large or small. What does change looks like? It looks like always questioning how you do things. It means always striving to bring improvement. It looks like questioning and stretching the people who work for you, who work with you and questioning even your company's fundamentals on an on-going basis. It should also mean soliciting your client's for feedback for your improvement.

When we question, re-examine and observe closely our daily work, we can determine if we're excelling in that work and identify areas for improvement. When we hire young workers who lack experience but bring a fresh perspective, this is one critical way to stay current. In other words, inviting change is a means of combating complacency and always striving to be the best with your company. It means always being on the lookout for ways to improve and taking the action to insure change and growth.

This concept is so critical, because change is inevitable, why don't we take it on fully, and actually effect change ourselves instead of passively waiting? We who've risen to the top ranks in a company are the best equipped to know our strong suits, our own abilities, our clients and our own corporate cultures and it's our job to steer the change coming our way and in this way we make it more manageable. If we maintain an open mindset that doesn't fear change but invites it head-on, we're setting our company up for continued growth and re-invention. That's what keeps your organization at the top. That is what will make your company, and your career a success.

In the end whether you are starting your career or hoping to gain great positions in executive management you can bet on two things. First, yourself, with all the skills, strengthens, and experience you bring. Second, your attitude when you are faced with the type of change or adversity. How you handle this will be either your greatest failure your most triumphant success.

EPILOGUE

"The highest reward for a person's toil is not what they get for it but what they become by it."
—Unknown

So recently I found myself in the Salt Lake City airport waiting out a three-hour layover—the same airport where it all began for me with that flight to California. I was flying back to the East coast at about two the morning. There I was walking through the airport with very few people around me. The emptiness allowed me to reflect on my career over the past 20 years. I imagined that I met myself at 23 and I said to her:

"Liza in about 20 years you will be traveling through here again. You will have started a couple of software firms, employed a good number of people and you will be highly successful in business. You will have lived in the Pacific Northwest but will have traveled to many places in the world before finally settling on the east coast. You will meet some amazing people on your journey who will help lead you in the right path but sometimes you will still take the wrong path. You will learn to learn from all the twists and turns life will throw at you and in the end you will be still be standing, as proud, brave and confident as you are now as a young women.

When you are the older me you will still believe that there is more ahead of you, you will continue to be the risk taker you have been your entire life. You will always innately know that there is more out there for you and you won't ever stop pursing your dreams. This is what allows you to keep imagining all you want in this life and shaping the life you want. As you depart from this airport to your new life remember always that your life will be blessed and God will always be with you!"

AFTERWORD

Last, I'm remembering a favorite quote:

"You must live in the present, launch yourself on every wave, find your eternity in each moment. Fools stand on their island of opportunities and look toward another land. There is no other land; there is no other life but this."
—Henry David Thoreau

I've always understood that I never wanted to just stand on that island. And here is one other Thoreau quote that is never far from my mind is:

"Go confidently in the direction of your dreams. Live the life you've imagined."

I can honestly say as I look out my bedroom window, my kitchen doors, over the front of my bicycle handlebars, or through the foggy water of my goggles, I am living the life I imagined and even though this is a very different life than the life I led in the past, and oddly at that point I was living the life I imagined also! Henry was right, if you go confidently, with certainty, in the direction that you know is right for you, on the road that leads you to whatever your goal is, you can't not achieve what is meant for you.

You will make it and you will achieve whatever it is you desire. There is no question that the road you are on, will take you somewhere. It is in your own wisdom that you need to ensure you are on the right freeway today and if you are not, get off and take the next exit. In reality, it is that simple.

ACKNOWLEDGEMENTS

How does a busy CEO move a book from an idea to a reality in her non-existent spare time? The answers here rest on the shoulders of a few key people and I'd like to thank them for seeing the dream of this book through to print. First, I'd like to thank Topher Morrison of KPI, for giving me the directive to "Get writing!" I also want to acknowledge that I've had the help of a very talented and patient ghostwriter and content editor, Francesca R. Kennedy. Francesca spent countless hours researching and discussing my chapters and then painstakingly took my writing and my ideas and wove them into the book that you're holding in your hands. Francesca lives on a sailboat in Florida with her husband, a young son, two parrots and two Labrador retrievers. She is a contributor to Cruising Outpost Magazine. She has worked for WCSC, Channel 5 news in Charleston, South Carolina and WPTV, Channel 5 in West Palm Beach Florida. She is an avid sailor and she enjoys competing in open-water swim races throughout Florida and the Caribbean. She has written a book on the topic of open water swimming for the novice.

There are also so many personal thanks I'd like to give. As I've mentioned throughout this book, I've been blessed by the support, guidance, direction and love from the many special women in my life. In addition to the women previously mentioned I want to acknowledge the following and show them my appreciation for the numerous ways in which they've showered love on me:

First, my aunties. Lillian McNatt who in her generous spirit faced tragedy that made her dig deep and show the world how brave she truly was and Elaine Fairborn who lives her life as an example of kindness to all and who, without a doubt is one of the most good-hearted women I know; and my Aunt Cathy "Cookie" Cisneros who is an example for all women with her strong, unapologetic sense of self. Her sense of humor is second only to the love she exudes to her family and friends. I'd also like to remember my deceased grandmother, Katie Cisneros, who taught me by example what it means to have a strong sense of family and I often hope to emulate her love of her family in mine.

I give a nod to my girlfriends, the very best women I know. These women are the ones that know most of my secrets. They've seen me through some of the greatest times and some of the biggest trials of my life. These women love on my daughters like the incredible mom's they are and each of them is absolutely extraordinary in her own world. I am privileged to be able to drink "Cosmos" and champagne with them and to call them my best friends. I am grateful to be able to share and celebrate with them all of my most important life moments. Jeanette Lineberry, Robin Kinerk, Rajpreet Gill, Ann Voves, thank you for everything!

I want to acknowledge my parents and thank them for the obvious, my upbringing. Collectively they were my "Anthony Robbins" and my "Dale Carnegie." My mother was my "Sheryl Sandberg" who unwittingly taught me to "lean in" by showing me how she made things happen in her life and her business career. Just as I hope to emulate a life my daughters want to follow, my parents did just that for me. I thank my father for being an amazing athlete and excellent business executive. He made me want to match his accomplishment in the office and on the running trail by completing a marathon. He continues to inspire me to be a better athlete, just like him. My father knows how I feel about him and although there is a long list of people who know and admire my father I will always be first in line with my admiration, respect and love for him. As I've shared with many people, my father is the best person I know. I mean it completely. For this I thank him.

My mother is more difficult to describe. You might even say she's a hard nut to crack mainly because she is a woman of so much change herself. She is a woman who grows discontent with her life from time to time so she shakes it up and affects change in response. My mother has been amazing and inspiring to watch as she's changed and grown. She became a college graduate after barely having the grades to complete high school. Today, she is an amazing artist and what I'd describe as a true Renaissance woman. She's accomplished all of this in spite of essentially being told she wasn't good enough to succeed by her father. In addition, my mother has taught me about being a woman of God and her devotion is to God is admirable. But the greatest thing I learned from her is there is no straight line to achievement. No matter how circuitous, you'll arrive at your destination as long as you keep on driving it forward.

Finally, the most important acknowledgement:

For from Him and through Him and to Him are all things. To Him be glory forever. Amen.
(Romans 11–36).

To Reach or Follow the Author
www.lizamariegarcia.com
Email: liza@lizamariegarcia.com
Twitter: LizaGarciaCEO
Facebook: https://www.facebook.com/liza.m.byrne
https://www.facebook.com/LizaMarieGarciaCEO
LinkedIN: Liza Marie Garcia
Instagram: lizagarciaceo